Fundamentals of Managing Reference Collections

ALA FUNDAMENTALS SERIES

Fundamentals of Managing Reference Collections

Carol A. Singer

American Library **Association** : Chicago 2012

Carol A. Singer is a reference and instruction librarian at Bowling Green State University in Bowling Green, Ohio. One of her primary responsibilities is coordinating the development and management of the reference collection. Her research has focused on reference collections and services, as well as government publications. She is the author of many articles and the editor of *Docs Prescriptions*, the newsletter of the Government Documents Round Table of Ohio. Singer earned her master's degree in library science at Indiana University.

Printed in the United States of America

16 15 14 13 12   5 4 3 2 1

Extensive effort has gone into ensuring the reliability of the information in this book; however, the publisher makes no warranty, express or implied, with respect to the material contained herein.

ISBNs: 978-0-8389-1153-2 (paper); 978-0-8389-9464-1 (PDF); 978-0-8389-9465-8 (ePub); 978-0-8389-9466-5 (Kindle). For more information on digital formats, visit the ALA Store at alastore.ala.org and select eEditions.

Library of Congress Cataloging-in-Publication Data
Singer, Carol A.
  Fundamentals of managing reference collections / Carol A. Singer.
      pages cm
  Includes bibliographical references and index.
  ISBN 978-0-8389-1153-2
  1. Libraries—Special collections—Reference sources. 2. Electronic reference sources—United States. 3. Reference books—United States. 4. Collection management (Libraries)—United States—Case studies. I. Title.
  Z711.S57 2012
  025.2'1—dc23

                                                                    2011044446

Book series design by Casey Bayer. Cover image © Gts/Shutterstock, Inc.

♾ This paper meets the requirements of ANSI/NISO Z39.48–1992 (Permanence of Paper).

This book is dedicated to my parents,
Richard M. and Eleanor W. Singer

Contents

 A downloadable, editable version of the Reference Collection Development Policy Template is available online at www.alaeditions.org/webextras/.

Preface

IN MANY WAYS, this is a difficult time to manage a reference collection. Most libraries still have large print reference collections that must either be maintained and updated, or drastically reduced in size. In some libraries, not only are many users ignoring the presence of the print reference collection, so are many of the reference librarians. When I realized that, after more than thirty years as a reference librarian, I was rarely going into the reference stacks except when I was preparing a class research guide or when I was weeding, I knew that the print reference collection was in trouble. Even though we know there are incredible, useful resources in the print collection, in most libraries the reality is that users and staff both prefer electronic resources.

However, simply providing these electronic resources doesn't guarantee that they will be discovered and used. One of the challenges in reference collection management is finding ways to ensure that the expensive electronic resources we acquire will also be used. In the quest to make their electronic resources used, libraries place virtual resources on lists and research guides, and even sometimes create virtual bookshelves to hold electronic reference books. Some libraries have purchased databases whose purpose is to identify appropriate sources and then link to the full text of those sources. Other libraries try to increase use by providing versions that are optimized for particular hardware, such as smartphones.

As the number of available electronic reference resources has expanded, print reference collections have become more of a legacy collection in many libraries. For years, we've seen articles in the library literature predict the demise of the print reference collection. For whatever reason, print reference is still alive, and many librarians continue to order print reference books, albeit at a slower rate. So, why would a reference collection manager want to continue purchasing print reference books? Despite articles that say all library users prefer online resources, there are still some users who prefer to use print resources. In some schools or colleges, teachers or professors require their students to use a certain number of paper sources when writing a paper. In some locations, Internet access may be nonexistent or unreliable. For some libraries, the cost of the electronic edition of a resource may be considerably more expensive than the paper edition, or the online version may be considered too expensive for the amount of use it would receive. This is particularly likely to be the case when a book, formerly purchased only once every five to ten years in paper, turns into an annual online subscription.

In some libraries, the legacy print collection may have turned into something of an albatross around the neck of the reference collection manager. Print collections, unless they are regularly weeded, can easily become bloated, unattractive, and discouraging to use. A lean print collection is more likely to be used simply because the useful materials are easier to find. However, if the library literature is any indication, many librarians are reluctant to weed a collection and will do so only when lack of space has become critical. Given practice, most librarians will find that weeding a collection can be a rewarding task, even though most librarians would never describe weeding as the most fun part of the job.

The aim of this book is to provide those who are responsible for managing reference collections with the knowledge and tools to perform this job efficiently and effectively. In most libraries, there is a shortage of both staff and money, so it's important that neither is wasted. This is true no matter the size or type of library, or the size of the budget. It's true even if the reference collection is composed entirely of freely available Internet sites. It still takes staff time to identify and maintain a collection of free sources.

This book is designed to explore the various aspects of designing, organizing, and maintaining both tangible and virtual reference collections. I have tried to include information that is applicable to any size library, from a one-person library to a major library system. I have also tried to include information suited to various types of libraries—public, academic, school, corporate, governmental, or organizational.

Acknowledgments

I HAVE BEEN extraordinarily lucky to work with many knowledgeable and dedicated people during the many years I have worked in libraries. They have been generous in sharing their knowledge with me. The discussions I have had with them have helped to form my view of how libraries and reference collections should be managed and how libraries—and librarians—should serve our users. I would like to thank the staff at the libraries where I have worked, including: the Delaware County District Library in Ohio; Rutherford B. Hayes High School in Delaware, Ohio; Indiana University; Wayne State College; the University of Nebraska at Omaha; Kenyon College; the U.S. Department of Energy; the National Agricultural Library; the U.S. Justice Department; and, of course, most particularly my friends and colleagues at Bowling Green State University, where I currently work.

Some of my friends and colleagues were gracious enough to agree to review one or more of the chapters in this book. Their comments and suggestions were extremely helpful to me. I would like to thank Linda Brown, Amy Fyn, Stefanie Hunker, Jeanne Langendorfer, Vera Lux, Coleen Parmer, and Linda Rich. My thanks also go to Elizabeth Wood and Stefanie Hunker, who drew my attention to articles or books that were useful in writing this book. The help I have received is typical of the wonderful people who work in the BGSU library. It would be difficult to find a better group of colleagues.

I would also like to acknowledge the chair of my department, Colleen Boff; Dean Kay Flowers; and Associate Dean (and later Dean) Sara Bushong, who were kind enough to grant me some research leave. This dedicated time was invaluable in allowing me to concentrate completely on writing this book instead of being focused on the everyday concerns of reference work.

I would like to thank J. Michael Jeffers of ALA Editions for suggesting I write this book. The staff at ALA Editions was great to work with and made this process easier than I anticipated.

Finally, I would like to recognize my friends and family, whose encouragement and support have been so important to me. While I was writing this book, they heard much more than they could possibly have wanted to know about the selection, management, and weeding of reference materials.

Reference Collection Fundamentals

Public libraries are useful to readers in proportion to the extent and ready supply of the helps they furnish to facilitate researches of every kind. Among these helps a wisely selected collection of books of reference stands foremost.

—A. R. Spofford[1]

Definitions

Before determining how best to develop and manage a reference collection, the definition and boundaries of that collection must be defined. In 1876, when A. R. Spofford wrote the passage at the beginning of this chapter, a reference collection was easily defined as a collection of reference books. In 1893, E. C. Richardson gave three definitions of *reference books*, one of which was "a book which is to be consulted for definite points of information (rather than read through), and is arranged with explicit reference to ease in finding specific facts." He also listed several points on which librarians generally agreed about reference books. One of these was that "a good collection of reference-books is fundamental to (a) the proper accumulation of a library, (b) to its effective use." Another point of agreement was that certain types of books were considered to be reference books, such as "general bibliographies, general encyclopaedias, general dictionaries of words, persons, places or things, atlases, and general indexes."[2]

This definition of a reference book remained relatively static for more than a century. In fact, the definition of a reference book in Stevenson's 1997 dictionary was similar. It defined a reference book as an "information book such as a dictionary, encyclopaedia or directory in which you can look things up."[3]

Today, a reference collection is rarely expected to be composed solely of books. Guidelines for the eleventh edition of the venerable American Library Association publication, *Guide to Reference Books*, the last edition available in print, stated, "Although the eleventh edition should continue to list primarily sources in printed format, those in machine-readable form should be included, recognizing the increasing importance of these sources."[4] This standard guide has now become an online-only resource, the Guide to Reference (www.guidetoreference.org), which includes reviews to both print and Internet resources useful for reference work.

Another guide to reference sources, the *American Reference Books Annual* (ARBA) was first published in 1970 as a guide to print reference resources. In 1993, ARBA began including CD-ROMs and, in 2002, Internet sites.

By this time, librarians were accustomed to using reference sources in a variety of formats. The definition of a reference work in the 2000 edition of *Harrod's Librarians' Glossary* reads, "sources of information (databases, abstracts, journals, books, etc.) which are used for answering enquiries in a library. Such items are not normally lent, but consulted only on the premises."[5]

The American Library Association's Dartmouth Medal, awarded to an outstanding reference work, was given to an online source for the first time in 2009, when the recipient was ABC-CLIO/Greenwood's Pop Culture Universe.[6]

In 2007, Michael Buckland wrote,

> The reference collection is composed of a set of resources selected to serve two needs:
>
> 1. Looking up or verifying factual data, often referred to as "ready reference"; and
> 2. Establishing an initial outline and *context* for any topic efficiently and effectively, especially determining the what, where, when, and who aspects of whatever is of interest.[7]

In 2009, an editor of *Choice* wrote, "Reference works serve as a go-to resource, a jumping-off point, a sure foundation for research. Though an exact definition remains elusive, most people think of dictionaries, encyclopedias, bibliographies, and the like."[8]

Paper or Electronic Resources?

As seen in the above definitions, reference materials are now commonly considered to include both paper and electronic resources. Few libraries have a reference collection that is exclusively paper or electronic. Most have a collection that includes both formats. Each format has its own strengths and weaknesses. In many libraries, there is still a large print reference collection, although this may be more of a legacy collection and receive little use. Even in libraries that still retain a large print reference collection, current acquisitions may be primarily online resources.

Sue Polanka wrote in 2008, "The reality is, print reference is dead, nearly dead, or never existed for many of our users, yet we still have patrons who need and prefer print."[9] Because of this diversity of user preference, many reference collection managers struggle over which format to purchase. The presence of a large legacy print reference collection may make a librarian conclude the easiest and most comfortable choice is to continue purchasing print copies, particularly for titles or series already present as a series of paper volumes on the shelves. One major factor in choosing to acquire paper or electronic resources may be cost. The print version may be substantially less expensive than the online version. It can be difficult deciding to purchase an online version of an encyclopedia that is three times as expensive as the print version. If the reference monograph budget is $10,000 and the average print reference book costs $250, the library could theoretically purchase forty reference books. However, if each electronic reference book costs $750, the library could theoretically purchase only thirteen reference books. In some cases, a book that costs $100 to $200 when purchased every few years in paper becomes an annual subscription of $3,000 or more per year for the online version. If the electronic resources are more expensive than the paper ones, the diversity of a reference collection could be compromised by a heavy reliance on online resources. Beth Juhl explains, "The most disturbing aspect of the transition to an online reference collection is the change from one-time monograph purchases to ongoing serial expenses. We have all lamented this at length, but I fear the long-term effect may be a loss of depth and variety in the reference collection."[10]

Of course, the pattern of cost differentials is rarely so consistent. Not all electronic reference books cost three times the price of the print edition. If the electronic book is purchased as part of an aggregated database, it's possible the online version may be cheaper. Also, if the online version is more heavily used than the print one, the cost per use may turn out to be less expensive for the electronic edition even though the actual price is higher. In some cases the library may be able to save money by using a free online equivalent, such as the Central Intelligence Agency's *World Factbook* (https://www.cia.gov/library/publications/the-world-factbook/). In addition to the initial cost of a resource, an additional consideration in a decision to purchase a title may be the potential cost of keeping either a paper or electronic resource up to date. While an electronic book may require an annual maintenance fee, a print one might require the purchase of pocket parts or transmittal sheets, plus the cost of labor to file the updates.

If the acquisition will be a continuing expense—which is the case for so many online resources—some libraries may worry the acquisition will turn into a future problem because the continuation of an adequate budget is uncertain. An article in *School Library Workshop* pointed out that not all school libraries have stable budgets. The author suggested purchasing online resources if the library could count on an adequate continuing budget, but "where support for the media center is never a sure thing, or where budgets are being slashed because of the economy, you will have to cover research needs by purchasing print to ensure you have material for students to use."[11]

However, cost isn't the only reason to prefer either print or online. One major factor in deciding which format to acquire is the preference of the library staff and library users. It's a false economy to purchase a cheaper print publication if nobody will use it. O'Gorman and Trott admit, "If we are seeing less use of print reference sources by library patrons, we are also seeing decreasing use of print reference collections by the staff . . . If librarians are going straight to the Web, then we certainly cannot fault our users for doing the same."[12] The lack of use of print reference collections isn't a new situation. In 2001, Margaret Landesman wrote, "Walking out to the reference stacks is starting to feel slightly spooky. There is seldom anyone there." She also noted that librarians serving on chat reference seemed to be perfectly comfortable answering reference questions from their offices, far from the print reference collection.[13] The decrease in the use of print reference collections may be more pronounced in certain subjects. David Flaxbart writes, "Let's be honest with ourselves. The use of printed reference works in the sciences has almost dropped off the meter these days."[14]

However, this lack of use of print reference resources may not be true in all libraries. Explaining why the lack of print tax publications was a problem, a Venice (Florida) Public Library reference librarian, Pat Maurer, indicates her library serves "a very computer-challenged older population."[15] This lack of computer knowledge for a significant user population might also affect the content of the reference collection. Lanning and Turner conducted a survey of school libraries to find whether their students preferred to use print or electronic resources. They found that, as the level of school increased, the preference for print resources decreased. Smaller schools and schools with small collection development budgets reported heavier use of print reference sources. The authors concluded, "In elementary schools, print reference resources offer ease of use and serve as great teaching tools of information literacy for students new to finding information. Print also offers affordability to schools on limited budgets. However, the preference at all levels is for electronic reference sources."[16]

Reasons for preferring online resources:

- Usually more than one person can use the resource simultaneously.
- The resource can be used 24/7.
- The resource can frequently be used away from the library.
- Online resources usually have more access points than paper resources.
- Aggregated databases frequently offer the ability to search individual titles and/or the entire collection, in addition to the ability to browse the collection.
- Online resources might sometimes be more accessible to those who have difficulty reading.
- Online resources don't take up space on library shelves.
- Some online resources offer attached audio files for full-text resources.
- Updates are integrated into the text, not pocket parts or transmittal sheets that might sit waiting for the main volume to be found so they can be incorporated.
- Online resources can't go missing from the shelves.
- Online resources are more easily used because the librarian doesn't need to leave the computer to access the resource.
- Online resources frequently offer persistent URLs that can be put in online guides and web pages, making them easier for users to access.
- Online resources are much easier to demonstrate in instruction sessions.

Reasons for preferring paper resources:

- The library may have poor or nonexistent computer or network access.
- The library may not be able to afford enough computers to provide adequate access for everybody who wishes to access online library resources.
- Some users may not be able to afford a computer at home, or all members of a household might have to share a single computer.
- Some users may still have dial-up access, too slow to use many of today's heavily graphic online resources.
- Some users may not like to use computers or may not know how to use computers.
- Paper resources can be used when the electricity is off.

- Paper resources can be used when the Internet is down or too busy to access.
- Content may disappear at any time from an aggregated database.
- Sometimes it's easier to find the desired information in the paper version.
- The online version might have a poorly designed user interface.
- Sometimes printing functions are difficult to use or are not allowed.
- Some libraries charge for printing, making printing sections of online resources prohibitively expensive for some library users.
- If the budget is tight, previously purchased print books are still available, unlike online resources that have been canceled.
- The library may be able to save money by purchasing a title that is issued annually only every two to three years—impossible when that title becomes part of an annual subscription.

Going Mobile

A recent Pew Center report asserted, "Cell phones now permeate American culture . . . The emergence of this pervasive mobile connectivity is changing the way people interact, share creations, and exploit the vast libraries of material that are generated for the internet." The study found that 82 percent of adults use cell phones and 24 percent use apps on their cell phones.[17] A 2011 Pew Internet report detailed cell phone ownership by age and also cell phone availability in the household by age, as shown in table 1-1.

TABLE 1-1
OWNERSHIP AND AVAILABILITY OF CELL PHONES BY AGE

Age in Years	Own Cell Phone	Cell Phone in Home	Total Availability
18–34	97%	49%	97%
35–46	92%	51%	96%
47–56	86%	29%	90%
57–65	84%	42%	90%
66–74	68%	24%	76%
75+	48%	27%	62%

Source: Zickuhr, Kathryn. *Generations and Their Gadgets*, p. 7.

Although this data includes all adults with cell phones—not only those who use apps on a smartphone—clearly libraries that serve segments of the population in which there is almost total penetration of cell phone usage should consider the implications for library services and collections. A survey administered for the Washington State Library revealed that 26 percent of respondents wanted the library to offer an application for smartphones.[18] This increase in the use of mobile technology is changing the way some library users interact with the library.

Doctors and medical students were early adopters of mobile technology. In 2004, Carol Tenopir estimated that between 35 and 50 percent of physicians and 80 percent of U.S. medical students were using PDAs. She surveyed the members of the American Academy of Pediatrics and found that approximately half were using PDAs, although they were using them mostly for personal use. However, more than 25 percent of those who responded to her survey were "definitely or probably" willing to search and access articles in the future with their PDAs.[19] A 2007 survey of students at Harvard Medical School revealed that 52 percent of medical students used PDAs and the most-used application was reference information, although the report didn't specify that the reference information was being supplied by a library.[20] Medical libraries have responded to this demand by providing databases of medical resources and medical information. For instance, the National Library of Medicine made PubMed for Handhelds (http://pubmedhh.nlm.nih.gov) available to researchers and clinicians. One of the reasons mobile technology caught on so quickly in the medical field is that it had so many advantages in a clinical setting. Joan K. Lippincott theorizes that this characteristic might make mobile technology attractive for adoption in other occupations with an emphasis on fieldwork such as "agricultural studies, environmental data collection, anthropological work, or social-services work in the community."[21]

The demand for library resources on handheld devices has been slower to develop in some other occupations and in the general public. However, as libraries and publishers have seen opportunities to serve those who use handheld devices, and as mobile technology users began to demand access to library services and resources, an increasing number of libraries have begun to offer mobile versions of their integrated library systems and mobile access to at least some other online resources.

Providing access to reference sources on handheld devices might be particularly attractive to libraries serving minority populations. An American Library Association Policy Brief states, "Through the continued adoption of mobile technology, library services can potentially engage traditionally underserved groups," and notes that ethnic minority populations typically had lower rates of home access to broadband service, but were as likely as whites to carry cell phones and access the Internet using their handheld devices.[22] This disparity in home access to broadband service by minority populations is further described in a National Telecommunications and Information Administration report, published in 2011, which found that only 49.9 percent of black, non-Hispanic Americans, 45.2 percent of Hispanic Americans, and 46.1 percent of American Indian/Alaskan Native non-Hispanic Americans used broadband Internet access in the home, as compared to 68.3 percent of white, non-Hispanic Americans.[23]

Some libraries have designed mobile versions of library websites to respond to user demand for library services and resources that can be used on handheld devices. In 2010, *Library Journal* conducted a survey of public and academic libraries and found that 44 percent of academic libraries and 34 percent of public libraries who responded to the survey were currently offering services designed for mobile devices. An additional 21 percent of academic and 22 percent of public libraries planned to offer such services. The mobile services most commonly made available by these libraries were a mobile layout or website (89 percent of academic libraries and 82 percent of public libraries) and a mobile-optimized interface to the library catalog (86 percent of academic and 87 percent of public libraries).[24]

Respondents to the *Library Journal* survey were asked to name other mobile services that were demanded by their library users. One of these was access to databases. Lisa Carlucci Thomas notes that an increasing number of commercial database providers were offering mobile-optimized interfaces.[25] A survey performed for the California Digital Library found that 53 percent of respondents wanted to be able to search library databases using a mobile device either "frequently" or "occasionally," while 46 percent answered that they would never search library databases on a handheld device.[26] Participants in the survey were asked, "Where do you find academic content to read on your mobile device?" The most commonly used sources were: online databases (67 percent), Google Scholar (43 percent), web searches (40 percent) and the library catalog (39 percent).[27]

Thomas also notes that some of the problems that prevented offering electronic books for mobile devices were "limitations of digital rights management, restrictive (or nonexistent) lending rules, exclusive platforms, and noncompatible file types."[28]

A 2010 report, written for the California Digital Library, lists the most significant barriers to using mobile devices with the Internet:

- Screen size too small (47 percent)
- Load time too slow (46 percent)
- Formats such as PDFs are difficult to read (41 percent)
- Formatting on web pages (40 percent)[29]

Despite the barriers that must be overcome, mobile-optimized library services and collections are increasing. In 2011, Joe Murphy predicted, "the roles of mobile devices in information discovery and engagement are expanding with no end in sight. Librarians exploring this shift now are doing more than reacting to a trend; they are preparing for the future."[30] Marshall Breeding asserted, "Libraries need to rapidly rally to deliver content and services to mobile users. The adoption of mobile devices in the general population of library users has reached a critical threshold. The increasing preference to access resources by small mobile devices ranks as one of those trends that libraries cannot afford to ignore."[31]

Defining Boundaries

The question that must be answered by anyone who's administratively responsible for a reference collection is: How do I define the boundaries of my reference collection? It's easy to see the boundaries of the tangible portion of the reference collection, but more difficult to determine which of the available virtual resources are also considered a part of the reference collection.

When determining these boundaries, libraries may consider virtual resources to be a part of the reference collection. One of the most common ways to define an online resource as part of the reference collection may be that it was paid for by the reference budget. A database might also be considered a reference resource because of the type of materials included in it, such as indexes, encyclopedias, dictionaries, statistical data, maps, etc. The item could be considered to be a reference material because it is the replacement for a print resource that was part of the reference collection.

Librarians also answer reference questions with print resources that are not part of the reference collection. If this happens often, the resource may be moved into the print reference collection. What indicates that an electronic resource has moved into the virtual reference collection? What designates something as belonging to the virtual reference collection? How is the virtual reference collection separated from the virtual nonreference collection, assuming such a category exists? There are those who say that anything online is a reference item, for all practical purposes, because it can be used for reference work.

Although it may be true that anything online might be used for reference, if something is categorized as part of the reference collection, it must be collected in some fashion that can be discovered and accessed by library staff and users. This may be accomplished by various methods. Virtual reference sources may be included in one or more lists of resources on a library website, included in a database of reference resources, incorporated into subject guides, or organized in a visual fashion, such as a virtual representation of books on library shelves.

Defining the Boundaries of a Print Reference Collection

The physical reference collection commonly occupies some of the most valuable real estate in a library, near the main entrance. In many libraries the space occupied by the reference collection was originally designated as such when the building was constructed. Over the years, some of the space allocated to the reference collection may have been reallocated, with libraries frequently removing portions of the tangible reference collection so additional computer workstations could be installed, making the virtual reference collection and other online resources more accessible. Some of the resources that have frequently been removed as part of this process (and as the content of reference collections has changed over time) include card catalogs, index carrels or shelving, telephone directories, college catalogs, vertical files, cabinets filled with company annual reports, and CD-ROM workstations. In some libraries, sections of reference shelves have been emptied and removed when the collection was downsized, perhaps as a result of the replacement of print resources by electronic ones.

Print reference collections still commonly include specialized collections in addition to the main shelves. These specialized collections may include dictionary or thesaurus stands, atlas stands, map cases, ready reference collections, indexes and abstracts, CD-ROM cabinets, or other auxiliary units. These collections are usually made up of items that receive heavy use or items that are awkward to put on the regular reference shelving. Oversized atlases are considerably less awkward to house and use if they are placed in special atlas stands. Maps are frequently oversized, making them very difficult to manage unless they are housed in special map cases. Some items are more conveniently placed in file cabinets in order to prevent them from being damaged or lost, such as pictures, annual reports, local history clippings, or pamphlets. Language dictionaries and thesauruses may be placed on special stands for the convenience of both library staff and users.

Ready reference collections are meant to segregate a group of resources that are frequently used by the reference desk staff. Because of their purpose, they are usually found near the reference desk. In many libraries, these print collections have gotten smaller as the function they perform is more commonly provided by online resources. Nevertheless, the ready reference collection remains a common feature in most libraries that still have a reference desk. Many of the sources found in a ready reference collection are books that are intended to provide quick answers, such as language dictionaries, almanacs, statistical compendiums, style guides, directories, chemical handbooks, biographical dictionaries, gazetteers, and similar publications. Unfortunately, like the rest of the reference collection, ready reference collections tend to become bloated as new materials are added and books that are no longer heavily used aren't removed.

Indexes may be shelved on separate shelving or intermixed with the rest of the reference collection. In many libraries, current indexes have been replaced with online equivalents, so the remaining indexes may be a legacy collection of older volumes that predate the time period covered by online databases, and receive little or no use. However, many reference librarians are reluctant to remove these older indexes from the reference collection because there is frequently no online equivalent, an occasional person might wish to consult them, and it can be difficult to determine which volumes of an index should be requested from an off-site storage facility when the rare researcher wishes to consult particular years. Because of these reasons, many research libraries choose to retain these older volumes. The reality, in some libraries, is that older indexes take up a considerable amount of space and receive virtually no use. In some libraries, these shelves of older indexes function primarily as sound and space barriers between tables of users.

A print reference collection, including a variety of specialized collections, still exists in most libraries. The collection may have diminished in size as the reference collection has become dominated by online resources, but it still demands significant time and attention in order to maintain it, even if the bulk of the use has shifted to the virtual reference collection.

Defining the Boundaries of an Online Reference Collection

It is much more difficult to define the boundaries of an online reference collection. The online resources available in a library might include databases of books and serials, but also such formats as videos, images, audio and video files, interactive maps, data sets, digitized 3-D objects, games, and so on. How many of these online resources can be considered a part of the reference collection? One method of determining this would be to see if each online resource fits the definition of *reference* as "sources of information (databases, abstracts, journals, books, etc.) which are used for answering enquiries in a library."[32]

Some online resources are simply online versions of print reference materials. This category would generally include indexes, some of the books and serials, some of the images, and at least some of the maps. Print indexes and abstracts have traditionally been shelved in the reference collection, and most librarians would consider index databases to also be part of a virtual reference collection. Online equivalents of reference books—such as encyclopedias, dictionaries, book or media reviews, directories, handbooks, manuals, or statistical compendiums—would probably be considered to be a part of the reference collection. As long as the online source is simply an equivalent to a print reference item, most librarians would probably be willing to designate the online resource as part of their reference collection.

It's increasingly common for a database that indexes text sources to include at least some full text. The equivalent print index would usually be considered a part of the reference collection, but the print publications that were indexed were probably not shelved in the reference collection. Now, both the index and the full text may be available in the same database. Blankenship and Leffler write, "While a collection of journals in the print world would not be part of a reference collection, it is easy to see how the lines between reference and serials collections are merging in the online environment. Many library users see online journal indices and full-text journal aggregators as similar tools."[33] In addition to databases that include full-text articles, libraries frequently provide access to databases of other types of full-text resources. Databases of full-text nonfiction books might be fairly easily considered to be a part of the reference collection because, due to the available searching capabilities, they might be usable for reference work. For instance, a database of scientific books might be used to search for information about specific chemical processes or laboratory procedures, even though the books that include the information were not intended to be used as reference books. Not all librarians would consider a database of fiction books, poems, short stories, speeches, or plays to be part of the reference collection. However, they might be used to identify a quotation.

A database whose title appears to define it as a reference resource might include additional resources or functions that would not be included in a print reference collection. Online encyclopedias may include audio and video files, games, exercises, stories, and many other inventive features, particularly if the database was intended for use by children. A directory might allow a researcher to create a list of companies and then print labels or create a spreadsheet of information about those companies.

A database that at first glance would not be considered part of a reference collection might include features that could make it useful for reference work. A database of music recordings might include a glossary of musical terms or a biographical dictionary of composers and musicians. A database that is primarily articles from popular magazines about health and medicine might also include entries from family medical guides or the text of prescription drug inserts. A database that is composed primarily of videos of theatrical performances might have a search engine that allows the user to compile a list of performances by director, lyricist, actor, costume designer, or choreographer. Some print reference sets include indexes that offer some of these capabilities, but rarely do they allow for such search sets to be cross-indexed as could be done in an online resource.

In addition to those online resources for which the library pays, there is a very large number of resources freely available on the Internet. Clearly some of these are reference sources. A database that indexes articles, such as ERIC (www.eric.ed.gov), PubMed (www.ncbi.nlm.nih.gov/pubmed/), or AGRICOLA (http://agricola.nal.usda.gov) are simply free versions of databases that many libraries acquire as a paid subscription. Some online sources are digitized or transcribed versions of a print reference book, such as *Roget's International Thesaurus of English Words and Phrases* (www .bartleby.com/110/) or the Central Intelligence Agency's *World Factbook* (https://www.cia.gov/library/publications/the-world-factbook/) . Others are similar to print or online subscription reference resources. This category might include such titles as the Internet Movie Database (www .imdb.com), OneLook Dictionary Search (www.onelook.com), or the U.S. Postal Service's Zip Code Lookup (http://zip4.usps.com/zip4/). Other online resources would be difficult to replicate in a print source because of the size of the database. A few examples of this type of site are the U.S. Census Bureau's American FactFinder (http://factfinder2.census.gov), the U.S. Department of Agriculture's National Nutrient Database for Standard Reference (www.nal.usda.gov/fnic/foodcomp/search/), and the Internet Archive (www.archive.org).

Because online resources often include both reference and nonreference materials and allow for nonreference materials to be more easily used for reference work, it's difficult to define some as reference and others as nonreference. In fact, some librarians believe that any online resource could be considered to be a reference source. Margaret Landesman writes, "The ability to search full text, though, turns every collection of online texts into a reference collection and provides an automatic concordance for every title. Titles can no longer be tidily separated into 'reference works' and 'general collection.'"[34] There's no universal rule that defines the boundaries of a virtual reference collection. Each reference collection manager must make this decision for her own collection.

How do librarians mark the boundaries of an online reference collection? They mark them by placing online resources in some type of organized collection. If the list of online reference resources is fairly small, the simplest method might be to compile them into a list that resides on the library's website. However, as the number of available databases, electronic books, and other resources multiplies, it becomes necessary to find more complex ways to define what materials are included in the reference collection and to provide effective methods to discover what resources are available. (Chapter 9 explores some of the ways librarians have used to provide ways to discover and access virtual reference collections.)

NOTES

1. A. R. Spofford, "Works of Reference for Libraries," in *Public Libraries in the United States of America: Their History, Condition, and Management; Special Report* (Washington: Government Printing Office, 1876), 686.
2. E. C. Richardson, "Reference-Books," *Library Journal*, July 1893, 254.
3. Janet Stevenson. *Dictionary of Library and Information Management* (Teddington: Peter Collin Publishing,1997), 130.

4. Robert Balay, ed., *Guide to Reference Books*, 11th ed. (Chicago: American Library Association, 1996), xxi.
5. Ray Prytherch, comp., *Harrod's Librarians' Glossary and Reference Book*, 9th ed. (Aldershot: Gower, 2000), s.v. "reference material."
6. Mary Ellen Quinn, "Inside the 2009 Dartmouth Medal Winner," *Booklist*, May 15, 2009, 66.
7. Michael K. Buckland, "The Digital Difference in Reference Collections," *Journal of Library Administration* 46 (2007): 88.
8. Carolyn Wilcox, "The Reference Roller Coaster," *Choice* 47 (November 2009): iv.
9. Sue Polanka, "Is Print Reference Dead?" *Booklist*, January 1 & 15, 2008, 127.
10. Frances C. Wilkinson and Linda Lewis, "Would You Like Print With That?— Will Electronic Reference Packages Supplant Print?" *Against the Grain*, September 2002, 24.
11. "Reference Question," *School Library Workshop*, Fall 2009, 15.
12. Jack O'Gorman and Barry Trott, "What Will Become of Reference in Academic and Public Libraries?" *Journal of Library Administration* 49 (May/ June 2009): 331.
13. Margaret Landesman, "The Cost of Reference," *Library Journal*, Nov. 15, 2001 supp., 8.
14. David Flaxbart, "Death of an Encyclopedia Salesman? The Fate of Science Reference Resources in the Digital Age," *Issues in Science and Technology Librarianship* (Summer 2004): n.p.
15. Michael Kelley, "Missing Tax Forms Cause a Headache for Librarians," 2011, www.libraryjournal.com/lj/home/889230–264/missing_tax_forms_cause_a .html.csp.
16. Scott Lanning and Ralph Turner, "Trends in Print vs. Electronic Use in School Libraries," *The Reference Librarian* 51 (2010): 214–221.
17. Kristen Purcell, Roger Entner, and Nichole Henderson, *The Rise of Apps Culture*, 2010, 9–11, http://pewinternet.org/Reports/2010/The-Rise-of-Apps -Culture.aspx.
18. Ahniwa Ferrari, *Electronic Resources for Library Users: A Survey by the Washington State Library*, 2011, 9, www.sos.wa.gov/quicklinks/EResource -Survey-Users.
19. Carol Tenopir, "Searching on the Run," *Library Journal*, Oct. 1, 2004, 32.
20. Joan K. Lippincott, "Mobile Technologies, Mobile Users: Implications for Academic Libraries," *ARL*, December 2008, 1.
21. Ibid., 2.
22. Timothy Vollmer, *There's an App for That! Libraries and Mobile Technology: An Introduction to Public Policy Considerations*. Policy Brief No. 3. Washington, DC: American Library Association, 2010.
23. U.S. Department of Commerce, National Telecommunications and Information Administration. *Digital Nation: Expanding Internet Usage* (NTIA Research Preview), 2011, 11, www.ntia.doc.gov/reports/2011/NTIA_ Internet_Use_Report_February_2011.pdf.
24. Lisa Carlucci Thomas, "Gone Mobile," *Library Journal*, October 15, 2010, 31–32.
25. Ibid.

26. Rachael Hu and Alison Meier, *Mobile Strategy Report: Mobile Device User Research*, 2010, 27, https://confluence.ucop.edu/download/attachments/26476757/CDL+Mobile+Device+User+Research_final.pdf?version=1.
27. Ibid., 28.
28. Thomas, "Gone Mobile," 33.
29. Hu and Meier, *Mobile Strategy Report*, 22.
30. Joe Murphy, "The Mobile Revolution and *The Handheld Librarian*," *The Reference Librarian* 52 (2011): 1.
31. Marshall Breeding, "The State of the Art in Library Discovery 2010," *Computers in Libraries*, January/February 2010, 33.
32. Prytherch, s.v. "reference material."
33. Lisa Blankenship and Jennifer Leffler, "Where Are the Reference Books?" *Colorado Libraries* 32 (Spring 2006): 12.
34. Margaret Landesman, "Getting It Right—The Evolution of Reference Collections," *The Reference Librarian* 91/92 (2005): 19.

FOR FURTHER INFORMATION

Disher, Wayne. *Crash Course in Collection Development*. Crash Course Series. Westport, CT: Libraries Unlimited, 2007.

The Handheld Librarian (blog). http://handheldlib.blogspot.com.

Johnson, Peggy. *Fundamentals of Collection Development and Management*, 2nd ed. Chicago, American Library Association, 2009.

M-Libraries: A Best Practices Wiki. www.libsuccess.org/index.php?title=M-Libraries.

Spectrum: Mobile Learning, Libraries, and Technologies (blog). http://mobile-libraries.blogspot.com.

Zickuhr, Kathryn. *Generations and Their Gadgets*, 2011. http://pewinternet.org/Reports/2011/Generations-and-gadgets.aspx.

2

Reference Collection Development Policies

SOME LIBRARIANS WONDER if a reference collection development policy is necessary, particularly if there is already a comprehensive collection development policy for the library. In some libraries, the collection development policy is an umbrella policy that covers all collections within the library. The reference collection may be explicitly and comprehensively covered within this policy. Having a single collection development policy that covers the entire collection is not uncommon in a smaller library, but many larger libraries have a general collection development policy and additional policies for the various specialized collections in the library or library system.

There are also librarians who think a reference collection development policy is a waste of time. They say that many librarians who write a reference collection development policy just file it away, never to be seen again. They believe librarians are much too busy to spend time producing a complex policy instrument that will never be used. A 2009 survey of academic and public libraries in New York found that 58.6 percent of respondents did not have a written reference collection development policy. Those who did not have a written reference collection development policy included 65.1 percent of the public libraries and 46.5 percent of the academic libraries.[1]

However, drafting a separate collection development policy to cover the reference collection can fulfill multiple purposes. A reference collection development policy serves as the basis for decision making by those who build and maintain the reference collection because it defines the purpose of the collection and describes the content of the reference collection, both what should be included and—just as important—what should not be included. Having a written record of the decisions that have been made about the purpose and scope of the reference collection can help ensure continuity when personnel changes. The policy can be used as a resource when justifying budget requests. A posted collection development policy serves as a resource to answer user questions about library policies concerning the reference collection. It can also be useful if materials purchased for the collection, or removed from the collection, are challenged by people inside or outside the library.

Daniel Liestman lists six reasons for having a separate collection development policy for reference:

1. The policy serves as a "systematic framework for maintaining balance" in the collection. He was particularly concerned about format and content.

2. The policy is helpful in controlling the size and growth of the collection.

3. The policy provides clear guidelines for what should be selected—particularly important, as most reference resources are relatively expensive.

4. The quality of the reference collection is a critical component in determining the effectiveness of the library's reference service.

5. Because reference is changing so rapidly, it helps to have a statement that can be frequently updated to reflect those changes.

6. The reference collection should receive special attention, as it often provides a user with a first impression of a library.[2]

The process of writing a reference collection development policy is as important as the policy itself. In order to write the policy, there must first be discussions about the purpose, scope, content, development, and maintenance of the reference collection. These discussions should involve the reference staff who rely on the reference collection in order to do their work, and also the staff who are responsible for shaping the reference collection, although there may be substantial overlap between these two groups. The more people who are involved in this process, the more time will be needed to resolve all the issues that must be considered before a reference collection development policy can be written. Even though this can be a long and sometimes contentious process, the result should be a much deeper and more comprehensive understanding of how reference services play a role in fulfilling the mission of the library and how the reference collection supports that role.

Liestman writes, "The actual process of creating a policy is beneficial as it forces the library staff to consider unspoken/unrecorded assumptions about the reference collection. In order to successfully manage a reference collection, a library's staff must possess a shared understanding of their reference philosophies as well as the users' current and anticipated information needs . . . Developing such a document provides the opportunity for those involved to come to a consensus about major goals for the collection and reference service."[3]

The reference collection development policy may be solely the responsibility of the reference department or a joint responsibility of reference and collection development. It might be considered an internal document that does not need to be approved by other organizational entities. In some libraries, the policy will need to be approved by the head of collection development, the director of the library, a committee within the library, or a person or committee outside the library. Lukenbill reports that school districts employ various methods of producing collection development policies. The policy might be written by librarians or the library supervisor. However, in some large school districts, the governing board may appoint a committee to write the collection development policy if the project is expected to be difficult and politically sensitive. The policy may need to be reviewed by various interested parties. There may even need to be a public hearing to allow people who live within the school district to have an opportunity to comment on the policy as part of the approval process.[4]

The Parts of a Collection Development Policy

A collection development policy may be fairly simple or quite complex, depending on the size and complexity of the library or library system. Because there are so many different kinds of libraries serving a variety of communities, the decisions made about which components to include in a reference collection development policy will reflect that diversity.

Sections that may be needed include:

- Purpose of the collection development policy
- Responsibility for collection development
- Purpose of the reference collection
- Target audience(s)
- Budgeting and funding
- Selection criteria

- Selection aids
- Preferred format
- Duplicates
- Preferred language(s)
- Circulation
- Treatment of specific resource groups
- Resource sharing
- Collection maintenance
- Weeding and reviewing the collection
- Policy revision

Purpose of the Reference Collection Development Policy

In this section, the purpose(s) of the reference collection development policy should be described. Why is the policy necessary? What will be included in it? A purpose statement for a middle school library might be:

> The purpose of the reference collection development policy is to establish general guidelines for the scope of the library reference collection in order to support the academic programs of the Margaret S. Whitlinger Middle School. This policy will establish procedures for the acquisition of new materials and the removal of materials, thereby insuring the proper development and maintenance of a current and useful reference collection.

A reference collection development policy from Iowa State University defines the purpose of the policy as to:

- Provide the guidelines needed to build and maintain a Reference Collection of consistent quality and usefulness.
- Clarify responsibility for building and maintaining the Reference Collection.
- Set parameters for the scope of the Reference Collection.
- Provide rationales for selection and retention decisions.[5]

A policy from Messiah College states, "This policy is designed to augment and complement the Library's general Collection Development Policy, specifically treating the reference collection. General guidelines on issues such as relevance, potential usage, timeliness, accuracy, language and format, currency vs. retrospective emphasis, and cost are addressed in the general policy."[6]

Responsibility for Collection Development

In many libraries, one person is administratively responsible for selecting materials, managing budgets, maintaining the collection, reviewing the collection, and the many other duties necessary to administer a reference collection. With the inclusion of both print and online resources in the collection, this has become more complicated—all the tasks needed to manage the print collection are still needed, plus those for the online collection. In a large library, the person who is administratively in charge of the reference department may also be responsible for managing the reference collection, or this responsibility may be given to another librarian. The organization of staff members responsible for developing the reference collection varies widely due to the type of library and the size of the library organization. (A more thorough exploration of staffing patterns is contained in chapter 3.)

A collection development policy from the Bridgewater Public Library in Massachusetts included the statement "Selection of new reference materials is the responsibility of the head of the Reference Department, with input from other members of the department and from libraries in the region."[7]

A reference collection development policy from California State University, Sacramento, states, "The responsibility for the selection and maintenance of the reference collections belongs to the heads of each department (Social Science and Business Administration, Education and Psychology, Humanities, Science and Technology) in coordination with the librarians responsible for selection in the various disciplines."[8]

The Monroe Township Public Library in New Jersey assigns responsibility: "While the Library Director has primary responsibility for developing and maintaining the reference collection, every reference librarian who staffs the Reference Desk is responsible for making recommendations for updating and expanding the collection. Public recommendation of titles for purchase is encouraged."[9]

A reference collection development policy for the University of North Dakota describes those responsible for the collection:

> The primary responsibility for the development of the reference collection rests with the Head of Reference and Research Services, in coordination with the Head of Collection Development. Important secondary inputs will be provided by the Assistant Head of Reference and Research Services and the reference-bibliographers. Faculty suggestions for materials supporting the curriculum will be encouraged. Final decisions on adding materials to or weeding materials from the collection and on location of materials within the collection are also ultimately the responsibility of the Head of Reference and Research Services."[10]

A 2009 survey of academic and public libraries in New York revealed that responsibility for the management of the reference collection was assigned to the head of reference in 44.4 percent of libraries, assigned to reference librarians in 30.8 percent, and to subject librarians in 7.5 percent.[11]

Purpose of the Reference Collection

In 2007, Michael Buckland wrote that a reference collection fulfills two needs:

1. Looking up or verifying factual data, often referred to as "ready reference"; and

2. Establishing an initial outline and *context* for any topic efficiently and effectively, especially determining the what, where, when, and who aspects of whatever is of interest.[12]

Of course, the stated purpose of the collection will vary depending on the type of library, the mission of the library, and the needs of the clientele served, in addition to the philosophies and goals of the reference staff, library administration and the library's parent organization.

A collection development policy for the adult reference collection at the York County Library describes the purpose of the collection: "The York County Library reference collection is selected and maintained to meet two basic goals: to provide answers to specific questions of any informational or educational nature from patrons' in-person or telephoned requests; and to provide back-up reference assistance to York County Branch Libraries and the Bookmobile."[13]

A reference collection development policy from California State University, Sacramento, states, "The purpose of the reference collection is to make available resources, regardless of format, that provide information related to the curriculum, campus research, as well as other sources required for a university library."[14]

The Monroe Township Public Library in New Jersey defines their reference collection: "The primary criterion for classifying any title as reference is utility in meeting the specific and recurrent information needs of users."[15]

A collection development policy from Morton Grove (Illinois) Public Library includes the statement "Whether the information is related to academic assignments, employment, business, health, consumer concerns or recreational pursuits, there is an expectation on the part of the Morton Grove public that the Library will either have the answer or know where to find it. The Library's aim is to provide the information resources to meet this expectation and need."[16]

Target Audience(s)

The primary audience for reference services and, therefore, the reference collection, may have already been listed in the section on the purpose of the reference collection. If not, it should be defined in this section. There may be audiences other than the primary one that will be served by the reference collection. A public library may exist to serve the citizens of a particular geographic location but may also find use by residents of neighboring library districts, by students of a local college or university, by people who are taking online courses from colleges or universities that are not local, by teachers at local public and private schools, by local businesses, or by employees of the various local governments. In addition to serving the university's students, faculty, and staff, a university library may also be used by many high school students and other local residents, including many of the same people who use the public library. Corporate, school, and government libraries may have more restrictive regulations about who is authorized to use their facilities. However, some government libraries—particularly state, provincial, or national libraries—may serve a broader clientele. In addition, some U.S. government libraries may be assigned at least some responsibility for answering requests made under the auspices of the Freedom of Information Act.

A statement about the target audience for the reference collection at a corporation is found in a collection development policy from the Huntsman Chemical Corporation (Chesapeake, Virginia): "The Reference Collection consists of books and materials frequently consulted by members of the R&D department."[17]

New Mexico State Library has a very different statement of clientele served: "The primary groups served by this policy are state agencies, libraries throughout the state, and citizens with information needs related to government."[18]

Budgeting and Funding

The policy should say both where the money comes from and how it is allocated. There may be a single budget from which all reference materials will be purchased. In some libraries the reference budget may be divided by format, so there may be budget lines for monographs, serials, standing orders, and databases. If the library has an approval plan, there may be a separate budget line for reference materials acquired through the approval plan. In some libraries there may be no separate budget line for reference. Instead, print reference materials may be purchased from a general monograph budget or from the budget lines assigned to numerous subject areas. Online resources may be purchased from a general local databases budget. (Additional information about budgets is found in chapter 5.)

Selection Criteria

The subject scope of the collection should be described, including the depth of the collection. Some libraries simply include a general statement about the subjects included in the collection. Other libraries prefer to list each major subject, with a detailed description of the types of materials included for each subject.

If there are subjects that are explicitly excluded from the collection, these should also be listed. These subjects may be irrelevant to the mission of the library or inappropriate for the age of the target audience, or the library intends to house certain types of reference materials in special collections or branch libraries. (Expanded explanations of selection criteria are contained in chapter 4.)

Common criteria for selecting reference materials, regardless of format include:

Relevance of content and current coverage of that topic in the collection: Is the resource relevant to the library's reference collection, and is that topic already sufficiently covered?

Authority of author, publisher, or database producer: Are these known for the quality of the materials they produce on this subject?

Accuracy: Does the content of the book or online resource include factual errors? Is important information missing?

Completeness: Is the content of the resource as a whole, and of individual entries, sufficiently complete for the purposes of the library's users?

Currency: If currency is important for this resource, will the currency of information meet users' expectations for this type of resource? Also, will the information be kept current in some fashion?

Age/user appropriateness: Considering the demographics of the library user population, is the content appropriate?

Accessibility: How easily will researchers, including those with disabilities and those outside the library, be able to find and use the information they want?

Geographic coverage: Does the information serve the geographic location of the library's users, if that is a consideration for the potential acquisition?

Preferred language(s): Is the content written in language(s) that are needed by the library's users?

Illustrations: Are the illustrations appropriate for the content and type of resource? Do they add to the user's understanding of the topic? Are they clear and easy to interpret?

Access points in other resources: Is the resource, or individual titles within the resource, referenced in databases or bibliographies to which the library subscribes?

Cost versus quality: Is the cost to the library appropriate for the quality and potential usefulness of the resource?

Common criteria for selecting online resources:

User interface: Is the user interface easy to use for the people who use the library's resources?

Branding: Are there adequate opportunities to brand the resource with the library's logo, name, or other desired information?

Customization: Is it possible to customize features that will make the user interface easier to use and more consistent with the user interfaces of other online resources provided by the library?

Search features: Are the search features easily identifiable and appropriate both to the content of the resource and to the needs and abilities of the library's users?

Available indexing: Are the searchable fields appropriate to the content of the resource and the needs of the library's users? Is the quality of the information in these fields accurate and complete? If the resource includes a controlled vocabulary, is it as detailed and comprehensive as necessary for the content of the database and the needs of the researchers?

Results display: Does the results display include the information needed to identify the indexed item and to determine if that title is likely to be useful for the researcher?

Availability of full text: What percentage of the indexed content of a database is available in full text? How easy is it to retrieve that full text?

Special features: Does the online resource contain special features that will enhance the usability or content of the database? Are those features appropriate for the content of the resource and for the library's users?

Ability to save, print, or e-mail results: Is it easy to save, print, and e-mail the indexed contents? Are there restrictions on these functions?

Ability to export citations: Are the citations of the indexed content easily exported to the bibliographic management software most used by the library's users, particularly any software supported by the library?

Updates/currency: Is the update frequency and format appropriate for the content of the resource and for the needs of the library's users? Is some of the indexed full-text content embargoed for a period?

Availability of downloadable MARC records: Are downloadable MARC records available for individual full-text titles in an aggregated database? Are these records included in the price of the resource, or are they available for an additional fee?

Usage data: What usage data is available? How can that data be accessed? Is it COUNTER compliant?

Remote access: Is the resource accessible to off-site users? Will the resource work with the remote access software program used by the library?

Mobile access: Does the resource provide a version that is optimized for mobile access? Is it optimized only for one particular type or brand of handheld device?

Cost models: What types of cost models are available? Will one or more of these fit within the library's budgetary procedures and budgetary limits?

Licensing: Are there elements in the license that may require additional negotiations, or may they need to be referred to an attorney?

Technical considerations: Does this online resource present additional technical challenges that may require the attention of the library's IT staff?

Common criteria for selecting paper resources:

Physical features: Are the binding, paper quality, and other physical features of the book of sufficient quality?

Visual qualities: Is the typeface easy to read? Are illustrations clear and appropriate for the content and the library's users?

Ease of use: Is the book well organized? Is the available indexing easy to use and appropriate for the content and the library's users?

Updates/currency: Are there provisions for updating the content, if desired or needed? Will the library need to subscribe to a service to receive transmittal sheets, pocket parts, or supplements?

Cost models: What cost models are available? Is the book available at a discount through the library's book vendor or other organization/service?

Selection criteria may be organized in other schemes. For instance, a collection development policy for electronic resources from Boston University organized criteria under five categories: Academic Need, Quality and Authority of the Resource, Usability of the Resource, Reviews and Trials, and Relation to Print.[19] A policy from Iowa State University also organized criteria into five categories, but chose Subject/Content Criteria, Access Criteria, Service Criteria, Format/Mounting/Storage Criteria, and Vendor/Contractual Criteria as section headings.[20]

Some libraries state criteria as questions that must be answered. For instance, the material selection principles from Pennsylvania State University contain a list of questions on various considerations, a few of which are: "What is the perceived quality of the information contained in the product? Is the information accurate? Is the information balanced, or does it present only a limited viewpoint? How comprehensive is the coverage of the information?" This document also includes a list of questions for resources that will be mounted locally, such as, "What is the size of the database relative to the storage capacity available? Do we need to buy more memory or additional hardware? If not, how long will it be before we have to upgrade?"[21]

Selection Aids

Note what major selection aids are used to select reference sources. This could include databases, such as the Guide to Reference (www.guideto reference.org); journals, such as *Booklist*, *School Library Journal*, or *Choice*; or books, such as the *American Reference Books Annual*. (A more complete list of general selection aids is found in chapter 4.) Libraries that specialize in one or more specific subjects may also use scholarly journals or trade journals that include reviews for reference materials in those subjects.

Preferred Format

Some libraries include a statement about the preferred format for the reference materials in the collection. A library might prefer electronic or print for all materials, or it might prefer one format for most materials but another format for certain types of materials. Preference for one format over another may vary, depending on the respective cost of different formats if the same title, or comparable information, is available in more than one format. If many users of the library rely on online access to information, that may be more important than the greater cost of an online resource, assuming that this will result in a lower cost per use even though the total cost will be greater. On the other hand, if a substantial number of users are averse to using computers, the policy may state that certain types of reference sources should be purchased in print or in both paper and electronic formats. (A discussion of the advantages and disadvantages of print and electronic formats is found in chapter 1.)

Some libraries may prefer to acquire some types of materials in microform, CD-ROM, or other formats.

This example of a preferred format statement appeared in a collection development policy from Florida Atlantic University: "The Libraries prefer to acquire materials in electronic format if available and deemed appropriate to provide improved access to all campuses or to enhance the Libraries' current collection."[22]

Duplicates

Reference materials tend to be expensive, so a library might wish to include a statement that addresses which, if any, resources should be purchased in duplicate. If there is a policy that covers all potential duplication in the reference collection or collections, there may only need to be an umbrella statement to cover this policy. If the reference collection manager will make such decisions on a case-by-case basis, this section of the collection development policy will reflect that practice.

Some libraries continue to purchase both print and online versions of a title in order to ensure availability if the library cancels the subscription to the online version or if the online version becomes unavailable for other reasons. When libraries began to replace print titles with online equivalents, this was a more common practice. As libraries have continued to replace print titles with electronic resources, many have ceased to purchase paper duplicates because they are unable to afford purchasing identical reference materials in multiple formats. In addition, some librarians have decided to rely solely on the online resource because they believe the online resource would most likely be canceled only if the level of use fell so much that the resource was no longer needed, in which case the library would no longer need either the paper or online copy. Some librarians also believe it would be useless to purchase a paper copy because their users wouldn't be willing to use the resource in paper, even if the online version was no longer available. Another reason for not purchasing duplicates is that this practice carries too high an opportunity cost because it means that some other unique title can't be acquired.

Some libraries purchase a duplicate in paper or microform to serve as an archival copy of issues of a serial publication. This is more likely for a source such as monthly stock market or bond market reports. It's a practice that was more common when such publications were purchased in paper. As libraries have replaced these with online resources, the archive is more likely to be a component of the online resource.

The policy in many libraries is to avoid the purchase of duplicate copies of paper items, although some continue to purchase multiple copies of certain heavily used titles, such as style guides, dictionaries, or thesauruses. One justification for purchasing an online format for a heavily used reference source is to allow simultaneous access by multiple users. In certain cases, the library may prefer to continue purchasing duplicate paper copies. For instance, if a style guide is issued every five years, a library might habitually purchase five copies at a total cost of $500 to $1,000. If the online version of that title is an annual subscription of more than $3,000, the library might choose to purchase multiple paper copies. However, that same library might instead decide to acquire the online version, believing that usage would increase to the point that cost per use would be equal to or lower than the cost per use of the print version.

A library system with multiple branches may also want to include a statement about the purchase of multiple print copies to be housed in various branches or departments. The library might prefer to instead purchase an online subscription that could be accessed from all branches or departments.

A collection development policy for Florida Atlantic University states, "Duplication of the print and electronic versions of a resource are generally discouraged but will be considered on a case-by-case basis."[23]

The Morton Grove (Illinois) Public Library defines responsibility for coordinating duplication in reference collections: "Selection of reference materials for Adult Services and Youth Services is coordinated so that no unnecessary duplication will occur, and so that the content of each reference resource is appropriate to the needs and educational level of its users. The Head of the Children's Department and the Reference Coordinator will consult each other regarding the selection of reference materials which may be appropriate to both departments."[24]

A reference collection development policy from the University of Georgia included this recommendation about duplication between reference collections: "Duplication of materials between the two Reference collections and the Law School should be kept to a minimum. Likewise, duplication of material in the stacks should be weighed carefully before deciding to add a second copy. Titles issued by the Government Printing Office should be searched carefully to minimize duplication from the depository collection."[25]

Preferred Language(s)

Many reference collections are composed primarily of materials in a single language, except for the inclusion of dictionaries in other languages. However, if there are significant user populations who read other languages, it may be necessary or desirable to collect reference materials in additional languages to serve these library users.

A reference collection development policy from the University of North Dakota includes the following statement: "In selecting ready reference tools, priority will be given to materials in English, with foreign language materials selected only if they are superior to or complement the English works available. If, however, the work supports the curriculum or is necessary for research purposes, no discrimination will be made on the basis of language."[26]

A collection development policy from the University of Louisville states, "The print reference collection includes the standard adult encyclopedias in English, and usually one new set is ordered annually. There is at least one encyclopedia set in Russian and each of the major European languages."[27]

Circulation

The print materials in most reference collections don't circulate. However, this is not universal. If some or all print reference materials circulate, that should be stated in the reference collection development policy.

Treatment of Specific Resource Groups

There may be some types of reference sources that require a separate statement. It would be cumbersome to list every type of reference source and whether it should be included in the reference collection, but it may be necessary to list some classes of resources that must be included or should not be purchased for the reference collection. For instance, the policy might declare that the library will purchase almanacs, yearbooks, and encyclopedias only for certain geographic areas. A list might be included of major atlases and gazetteers, with a schedule that details how often each should be purchased. The policy could include a statement about what type of examination preparation guides or quotation books should be purchased. There might be a list of types of reference materials that are no longer included in the collection, particularly if these resources were formerly purchased for the collection. For instance, a senior vice president from Zondervan notes that libraries were purchasing fewer concordances of the Bible because of the availability of electronic full text alternatives.[28] Liestman notes that most college reference collections don't include "'how to' guides, *Cliffs Notes*, travel guides, genealogy materials, vertical file materials, and used car price guides."[29]

A reference collection development policy from the University of Notre Dame states that their policy is to purchase the latest editions of almanacs, annuals, and yearbooks, and to keep up to nine previous editions.[30]

The Huntsman Chemical Corporation library has an example of a statement that excludes certain types of materials from a reference collection: "Since the cost of maintaining comprehensive up-to-date general and business reference collections would be prohibitive, the Library will rely on the wide range of information sources available through online services for answering these types of reference questions from all departments of the corporation."[31]

A statement may be needed to explain that certain subjects will be included in a special library's reference collection. For instance, "Music: Basic, general sources only (More extensive and advanced material is housed in the Music Library of Tufts University)."[32]

Resource Sharing

For some libraries, resource sharing has long been a consideration in the development of the reference collection. Library systems have frequently attempted to limit duplication of reference sources among the various branches, substituting a system of referring questions to other branches or contacting another branch for assistance with a reference query. Much of the resource sharing within a library system is accomplished by subscribing to online resources that can be used by all branches. The ability to share online resources among branches can be a powerful incentive to acquire an online resource as a substitute for a title that was previously purchased in paper.

Libraries in close proximity have sometimes made agreements for cooperative collection development, combined with a plan to provide mutual reference assistance. These plans didn't usually include lending a reference book to the other library, but instead involved photocopying or scanning pages from a reference book to send to the other library, or reading a short passage over the telephone.

Resource sharing has become increasingly important in the development of reference collections as a greater portion of most collections is composed of online resources, partially or wholly acquired through a consortium. Some materials acquired through a consortium may be chosen by the consortium, so that reference collections throughout the consortium contain a more uniform group of electronic resources, which diminishes the individual character of the collections. If the library also acquires locally chosen online reference sources, decisions about what should be acquired locally will be influenced by what resources are available through the consortium. In addition, the money that was sent to the consortium will decrease the amount of money that remains to purchase locally chosen reference materials. On the other hand, a library consortium can usually negotiate far superior prices for online materials than what individual libraries could achieve. This allows the library to provide a greater variety of online resources to its users than would have been possible with only local licensing. (Further discussion of the role of consortia in library reference collection development is found in chapter 8.)

Collection Maintenance

There are many tasks involved in the maintenance of both print and electronic reference collections. Because of this, many libraries divide these tasks among a number of people. (Further information about collection maintenance is contained in chapter 6.)

Weeding and Reviewing the Collection

A reference collection must be regularly reviewed, to determine both what materials should be weeded as well as what sections of the collection need to be expanded or updated. Many librarians are reluctant to weed, for a variety of reasons. Some librarians hesitate to weed materials that are considered to be standard sources, are still in excellent physical condition, cost a great deal when purchased, or include information that is still perfectly usable. It can also be difficult for busy librarians to find the time for a task that can be tedious and disagreeable, causes a great deal of work for members of the library staff, doesn't have a deadline, and can create bad publicity for the library.

This potential for bad relations with users is one of the reasons it is important to have a section on weeding as part of a reference collection development policy. If weeding decisions are challenged, the library is able to demonstrate that decisions to remove materials from the collection are based on a statement of policy, not simply a spur-of-the-moment decision.

Part of this policy should identify who is responsible for planning and administering this task, what other people or departments will be involved, and how often this should be done. Remember, this document expresses policy, so there will also need to be a separate document that describes the procedures for how the review will be accomplished.

This is a good place to state a rationale for weeding the reference collection. A frequent reason for weeding a collection is to keep the collection within a designated space. Another reason is to remove material based on content, physical condition, or lack of use. The criteria for removing materials from the reference collection generally mirror the criteria for selecting resources. (Considerably expanded information on weeding reference collections is found in chapter 7.)

A collection development policy from the Kitsap (Washington) Regional Library gives this rationale: "The Library's collection of resources, regardless of format, is continually and systematically reviewed and evaluated in light of how well individual titles and the collection as a whole are meeting the expectations and needs of the Library's customers." The policy states that one factor in the review of the reference collection is whether the book has circulated within the previous two to three years.[33]

A weeding statement from the Medical College of Georgia collection development policy reads: "Reference Collection weeding is based on the need for the newest information to be in a small, current, easy-to-use collection and does not mean that all weeded items are discarded; rather, many will be relocated to the circulating collection or Special Collections."[34]

A reference collection development policy from Southern Connecticut State University states, "The Reference collection is weeded periodically for the purpose of maintaining an updated and useful collection. Subject selectors are responsible for weeding the collection in their subject areas and all reference librarians participate in the deselection of the general reference collection."[35]

Policy Revision

As the content and format of the reference collection changes, the reference collection development policy should also be revised. A reference collection development policy that was revised five years earlier may no longer reflect the reality of a modern collection. Any reference collection manager is probably so busy with the activities necessary to develop and maintain the collection that revising policy documents is often postponed for a more convenient time. In many libraries, this time never arrives, and the revision is postponed again and again. To avoid a continual postpone-ment, the collection development policy should include a schedule for how often the policy should be reviewed and should name who will be responsible for seeing that this is accomplished.

NOTES

1. Jane Kessler, "Print Reference Collections in New York State: Report of a Survey," *Journal of the Library Administration and Management Section* 6 (March 2010): 36.
2. Daniel Liestman, "Reference Collection Management Policies: Lessons from Kansas," *College and Undergraduate Libraries* 8 (2001): 86.
3. Ibid., 88.
4. W. Bernard Lukenbill, *Collection Development for a New Century in the School Library Media Center*, Greenwood Professional Guides in School Librarianship (Westport, CT: Greenwood Press, 2002), 57–58.
5. Alice J. Perez, ed., *Reference Collection Development: A Manual*, RUSA Occasional Papers, Number 27 (Chicago: American Library Association, Reference and User Services Association, 2004), 4.
6. Ibid., 6.
7. Rebecca Brumley, *The Reference Librarian's Policies, Forms, Guidelines, and Procedures Handbook with CD-ROM* (New York: Neal-Schuman Publishers, Inc., 2006), 60.
8. Richard J. Wood and Frank Hoffmann, *Library Collection Development Policies: A Reference and Writers' Handbook* (Lanham, MD: Scarecrow Press, Inc., 1996), 103.
9. Brumley, *The Reference Librarian's Policies*, 60.
10. Perez, *Reference Collection Development*, 61.
11. Kessler, "Print Reference Collections," 35.
12. Michael K. Buckland, "The Digital Difference in Reference Collections," *Journal of Library Administration* 46 (2007): 88.
13. Perez, *Reference Collection Development*, 9–10.
14. Wood and Hoffmann, *Library Collection Development Policies*, 102.
15. Brumley, *The Reference Librarian's Policies*, 60.
16. Perez, *Reference Collection Development*, 8.
17. Wood and Hoffmann, *Library Collection Development Policies*, 360.
18. Ibid., 281.
19. Richard Bleiler and Jill Livingston, *Evaluating E-resources*. SPEC Kit 316 (Washington, DC: Association of Research Libraries, 2010), 72.
20. Ibid., 78–79.
21. Ibid., 99.
22. Brumley, *The Reference Librarian's Policies*, 144.
23. Ibid.
24. Perez, *Reference Collection Development*, 63.
25. Ibid., 64.
26. Ibid., 12.
27. Brumley, *The Reference Librarian's Policies*, 63.
28. "The Reference View," *Publisher's Weekly*, Oct. 5, 2009, 10.

29. Liestman, "Reference Collection Management Policies," 94.
30. Perez, *Reference Collection Development*, 39.
31. Wood and Hoffmann, *Library Collection Development Policies*, 357.
32. Perez, *Reference Collection Development*, 38.
33. Frank W. Hoffmann and Richard J. Wood, *Library Collection Development Policies: Academic, Public, and Special Libraries*, Good Policy, Good Practice Series (Lanham, MD: Scarecrow Press, 2005), 183–184.
34. Ibid., 193.
35. Brumley, *The Reference Librarian's Policies*, 64.

FOR FURTHER INFORMATION

Brumley, Rebecca. *Electronic Collection Management Forms, Policies, Procedures, and Guidelines Manual with CD-ROM*. New York: Neal-Schuman, 2009.
Hoffman, Frank W., and Richard J. Wood. *Library Collection Development Policies: School Libraries and Learning Resource Centers*, Good Policy, Good Practice Series, No. 2. Lanham, MD: Scarecrow Press, 2007.

3

Staffing Models for Reference Collection Management

IN A SMALL library, the question of what organizational model shall be used for reference collection management may be a moot point because there aren't enough staff members to necessitate a choice of centralized or decentralized staffing. In some libraries, the same person is in charge of reference and collection development, and that may also be the person who spends the greatest amount of time answering reference questions. This will probably be the person who is responsible for selection, maintenance, and weeding of reference materials.

In a larger library, responsibility for selection, acquisition, maintenance, and weeding of the reference collection will typically be divided up among not only a number of people, but also among several departments. The staffing for reference collection development and management in a larger library may be structured in a centralized or decentralized organizational model.

Centralized Staffing

In a centralized system, there is a single person—or perhaps a committee—in charge of selecting materials for the reference collection. This person may have administrative responsibility for all facets of developing the collection. The reference collection manager decides which materials will be purchased and in what format. This manager ensures the collection is maintained, plans and oversees the review of the collection, and coordinates the many tasks that are necessary to take care of the collection. In a large library or library system, there may still be a single person administratively responsible for the management of the collection, but the duties will be divided among a number of people because there are so many functions required to manage a large reference collection.

Having a single person in charge overall does not necessarily mean that there won't be another person who oversees the reference collection development activity. In some organizations, there may be one or more people in the administrative hierarchy who have the responsibility or capability to review the decisions of the person responsible for development. Among the people who may be charged with this responsibility are the director or assistant director of the library, the head of collection development, or the head of reference services. In addition to these people—or instead of them—perhaps someone outside the library has this responsibility. In some school systems, there is an administrator who can challenge books or other resources that the librarian wants to purchase, or who can review materials that the librarian wishes to remove from the collection. In a company, government agency, or other organization, there may be an administrator who has this type of oversight for the library.

In addition to people above the administrative level of the reference collection manager, there are frequently provisions for library staff members or users of the library to suggest titles that should be purchased, to request that materials be added to the collection on a particular subject, or to recommend that certain reference materials be removed from the collection. Certainly the reference staff will have a direct interest in the collection provided for their use because their ability to give information to library users is dependent on the reference collection. In most libraries the person in charge of the collection must seek the advice of others in order to have a sufficiently comprehensive knowledge of what resources are needed for the reference collection. Unless a reference collection has a very narrow focus, a single person rarely has such a broad subject background to make informed decisions about all the subjects included in a library reference collection.

Bergart and Lewis address the problem of a selector who must select materials in subjects with which he is unfamiliar, which can result in a collection that contains more resources familiar to the selector and fewer quality resources in subjects less familiar. They recommend the selector take an honest look at the gaps in his subject knowledge and ask for advice from experts who can recommend the best way to develop the collection in those areas.[1] This is particularly useful if a single person is responsible for the development of an entire reference collection.

Sometimes a committee is appointed to be responsible for selection. Committees are often used for selecting electronic reference resources because these resources are frequently expensive and the content of many databases is interdisciplinary or multidisciplinary. The committee may be composed of members from the collection development and reference staffs, or both, and may also include an electronic resources librarian or other specialist. This committee may also serve as the primary group to consider potential library involvement in consortial purchases.

Advantages of a centralized staffing model include:

- One person is in charge and therefore makes the development of the reference collection a priority.
- This person knows what budgets are available and tries to see that they are spent effectively.
- This person consciously tries to balance the collection.
- This person tries to be impartial and prevent the collection from becoming unbalanced.
- This person dedicates time for reading reviews of reference materials and seeks out new resources that are potential additions to the collection.
- This person oversees the maintenance of the collection.
- This person plans and administers a review of the collection to remove materials that are no longer needed.

Disadvantages of a centralized staffing model include:

- Only one person is in charge, and no one person can be sufficiently knowledgeable about all the subjects included in most reference collections.
- The success of this model is very dependent on the ability and hard work of that single person.
- It is essential for anybody ordering resources for use by the reference staff to be an active participant in reference work. However, being in charge of the reference collection may prevent this person from spending significant time answering reference questions.
- Because members of the reference staff lack responsibility for collection development, they may not be as engaged in the development of the reference collection, and valuable resources may not be identified for inclusion in the collection.

Decentralized Staffing

A decentralized system may be structured so that the person who co-ordinates the collection development for the reference collection is administratively in charge of the function or merely serves as a program coordinator, with little true authority.

In some large libraries, subject bibliographers are hired to purchase materials for particular subject areas. This may also include responsibility for choosing resources for the reference collection. In this case, the person with administrative responsibility for the reference collection may be primarily a coordinator. He may order materials that have been chosen by others, oversee maintenance of the collection, disseminate information, and perform other administrative tasks, but may or may not be involved in the decisions about what exactly to collect. In this type of organization, the person in charge of the reference collection may also participate in the decision-making process as a selector for one or more subjects.

In other decentralized systems, the subject selectors make suggestions to the reference collection manager, who has the final say in what should be purchased, although the expectation is that materials requested by selectors will be purchased as long as sufficient funds are available. This reference collection manager would be responsible for ensuring that the budget is allocated fairly. Whether or not the reference budget is formally allocated by subject area, everybody involved in the process would be aware of how the money has been spent and would be able to determine whether or not his/her subject area has been fairly treated. This wouldn't necessarily mean that the same amount of money is spent on each subject, because resources for some subject areas, such as business, law, and science, are frequently more expensive than those in such disciplines as education or the humanities. There may also be a difference in the level of use by subject area at an institution. For instance, if a university has a large engineering school and only a small English department, the engineering resources will most likely receive much greater use than those purchased for the English department. However, even if an exact balance can't be struck, the reference collection management can attempt to create an appropriate proportion, taking into consideration the cost, availability, and comparative use of resources in the various subjects included in the reference collection.

In either a centralized or decentralized system, one role the coordinator frequently plays is that of consensus builder. This is particularly important in a decentralized collection development system. In order for a decentralized system to work well, a high degree of collaboration among the participants is necessary. There will need to be agreement, or at least consensus, on how the various budget lines will be spent. In many libraries the expectation is that major decisions will be discussed by the reference and/or collection development staff and that a collective decision will be made. This is particularly true when staff members are debating whether to purchase a title that represents a significant percentage of the available money. A proposal to purchase an expensive title has the potential to result in a contentious discussion over whether this acquisition is the best use of the available budget. This type of conflict is more common when money is tight, but in most libraries there is rarely sufficient money for all the titles the reference or collection development librarians would like to acquire. When libraries used to spend most of the reference budget on print resources, most titles were a fairly small percentage of the total reference budget and more individual titles could be purchased. Because there might be quite a few new titles purchased for the reference collection, subject selectors were more likely to believe that money was fairly allocated. However, electronic resources are frequently more expensive than individual reference books and therefore represent a larger percentage of the available budget for reference materials. Even individual electronic reference books are often purchased as part of an aggregated database, which may be comparatively expensive. Debate over the prospective acquisition of any library resource that may cost $5,000 or $30,000 is likely to be more contentious than the decision to buy something that costs $150.

Consensus building is an important skill for the reference collection coordinator. Part of the process of building that consensus is to gather and disseminate information about the resources to be discussed so that all participants have the information needed to make an informed decision. Optimally, this information will be given to interested parties enough in advance of the meeting so there is time to consider it. Then, one or more meetings must be held so that everybody involved has the opportunity to make their concerns and opinions heard and to discuss the possible outcomes. This process is more likely to be time consuming if the item under consideration is expensive or if there is a debate over which of several items will be purchased with the available funds. So often, when several items are under consideration, each will support a different segment of library users. Because decentralized systems are more common in libraries large enough to have subject selectors or reference librarians who work with particular segments of library users, participants will have different priorities. The process of building consensus for expensive items among a group of people, who each represent a different constituency, has the potential to create turf battles. Planning—and sometimes a certain amount of tact—can help the reference collection coordinator minimize these turf battles and increase the likelihood of building the necessary consensus.

Advantages of a decentralized system include:

- People of varied subject backgrounds are more involved in collection development, which may result in a more well-balanced collection.
- There is still a coordinator to oversee the available budgets and ensure they are spent.
- Because people are more likely to be actively involved in the development of the collection when they have some responsibility, they are more likely to be aware of and have an interest in encouraging the use of the new resources.

- If collection development responsibilities are assigned to the entire reference staff, the collective experience in reference work can be a significant factor in building a comprehensive, balanced collection that will serve well for answering reference questions.
- If collection development responsibilities are assigned to subject specialists, the collective subject knowledge can be a significant factor in building a reference collection with depth in all desired subject areas.
- This organizational system works best when the participants respect one another and value a balanced collection.

Disadvantages of a decentralized system include:

- The coordinator is dependent on other people to oversee the available resources and order or request those that will be appropriate for the collection.
- The coordinator may or may not be in overall charge and have the authority to achieve the best balance possible in the collection.
- Building consensus, an essential process in a decentralized system, can be time consuming, and more meetings are generally needed.
- Reviewing the collection may be more difficult when responsibility for collection development is spread among many people.
- If subject bibliographers—who do not participate in answering reference questions—choose resources for the reference collection, some of the materials may not reflect the reality of the type of reference questions asked, even though they will reflect the scope of subjects that might be included.
- If reference librarians serve as subject bibliographers, in addition to being responsible for reference and instruction, they may be too busy to pay proper attention to collection development.
- A decentralized system might result in a collection that is not balanced if some selectors are more forceful than others in advocating for resources that support their subject areas within the collection.

Other Participants in Reference Collection Management

In a larger library, there will be other people who assist in the management of a reference collection. Some of the tasks that need to be done have been necessary for many years because they are part of the management of a print collection. Some such tasks include processing and shelving new books, keeping track of usage statistics, making book dummies, filing updates, arranging for binding or repair of damaged books, and taking weeded books to be processed, as well as many other maintenance and management tasks.

There are also staff members outside the reference department who play valuable roles in the management of a reference collection. The reference collection manager relies on those who work in acquisitions, serials, access services, preservation, and storage facilities. If the library belongs to one or more library consortia, the reference collection manager may also find the staff members who work at those consortia to be very helpful.

The maintenance of electronic reference collections can be time consuming and complex. Because of this, some libraries have added the position of electronic resources librarian. Whether this librarian is part of the reference or collection development department, she can be instrumental in developing an online reference collection by being responsible for vendor relations, bringing new resources to the attention of the relevant librarians, arranging for trials, negotiating licenses, ensuring appropriate branding of online resources, making changes to user interfaces, providing selectors with usage statistics, communicating with individuals and groups throughout the library, and performing many other tasks that are necessary in the life cycle of an online resource.

NOTE

1. Robin Bergart and Vivian Lewis, *Sudden Selector's Guide to Business Resources*, ALCTS/CMDS Sudden Selector's Series, #1 (Chicago: American Library Association, Association for Library Collections & Technical Services, Collection Management and Development Section, 2007), 66.

4

Selecting Reference Materials

SELECTING THE HIGHEST-QUALITY appropriate reference materials for a collection is one of the most important functions of managing a reference collection. As Alice Kroeger wrote in 1902, "Almost all books of reference possess defects as well as merits; it is difficult indeed to find one that is perfect."[1] This statement is just as true today as it was more than a century ago. Not only must the content of the collection be carefully selected, but the person in charge of the collection must constantly reevaluate what should be purchased and what should not be purchased. As Cassell and Hiremath wrote in 2006, "As the curriculum changes, the academic library must respond by adding new reference materials that will meet these new needs. Likewise, public libraries respond to the requests for information from members of their communities, reflecting their users' wide-ranging information needs and interests from educational and career interests to hobbies and leisure reading."[2] This process of responding to change is just as evident in school and special libraries, as the information needs of an organization change due to technological, societal, legislative, and curricular changes. Any type of library must respond to alterations in the demographics of its user population, such as a change in ethnicity, age or gender distribution, economic status, language skills, literacy levels, etc.

For many libraries, the number of individual selection decisions has decreased as reference collections have been transformed from paper to electronic resources because electronic resources are often much more expensive than books. Even if the reference budget has kept up with inflation, it doesn't purchase as many individual products. For instance, reference books are generally purchased as individual titles, while electronic reference books are often purchased as a group of books that have been formed into an aggregated database, resulting in fewer decisions about individual titles. This doesn't necessarily mean less time was spent making those decisions. A selector is likely to spend more time evaluating an expensive item than an inexpensive one. This is particularly true if the electronic resource includes many titles because the selector might need to spend a substantial amount of time evaluating individual titles in order to determine if the database as a whole will be a high priority for acquisition by the library.

So, even if the person in charge of the reference collection is making fewer selection decisions, it's important that those decisions be made effectively. The first step in developing the collection is to identify which subjects should be included in the reference collection. This should have been part of the process of writing a collection development policy. Once the reference collection manager is armed with this knowledge, he is able to determine which of the new tangible or virtual resources might fit into the reference collection. To do this he can read advertising brochures or other marketing information, read reviews, visit vendor exhibits at conferences, read blogs or electronic discussion lists, or listen to what other librarians have to say about which sources they've found to be valuable. Both reference and collection development librarians can be extremely useful in identifying additions to the reference collection. In fact, they can be the reference collection manager's eyes and ears at conferences. They can forward information about potential reference acquisitions they've heard about. Another way to find ideas for useful additions to the collection is to talk to new teachers, faculty, or other employees to see what resources they found most useful where they previously worked or went to school.

Once some potential new resources have been identified, the next step can be to examine these resources. In an ideal world, it would be possible to examine each item under consideration. However, that may not be practical, particularly for print materials. Some publishers are willing to send examination copies of reference books. This gives a selector the opportunity to decide if she wishes to keep the book for the collection. However, unwanted books must be shipped back to the publisher or vendor. If an electronic resource is under consideration, the library may be able to arrange for a company representative to demonstrate the resource at the library, or even better, the library may be able to set up a trial of the database. A trial can be effective particularly if it is available to the users who will be most likely to use the product if the library acquires it. Evaluative comments from end users can be a very valuable component of the decision-making process, although it can be difficult to convince end users to supply any extensive feedback. One factor that may hamper the usefulness of a trial is that the trial may only approximate the functionality of the database that will be available after the library subscribes—the trial database may not have the full content of the database, be fully customized, offer remote access, possess the ability to use open URL resolvers, or include other features that may make it a desirable addition to the reference collection. Nevertheless, a trial is frequently the best way of determining the likely utility of an electronic resource. Gary Schwartz, from Owatonna (Minnesota) High School, explains, "Before I spend money on a database, I try to have at least one teacher use it with his or her students. If there are glitches or the instructions/process is unclear, the problem will usually show up quickly. And by using this method, we can also gauge if the literacy level/instructional level of the information is on par with the level of the students"[3] A more comprehensive list of criteria for evaluating online resources is presented later in this chapter. Utilizing these criteria will help to ensure that a trial results in a critical evaluation of the resource.

Using Reviews of Books and Online Resources

When choosing reference resources, many librarians rely on reviews to gather information about potential acquisitions, even though reviews can be contradictory and vary in quality. Doug Johnson points out that reviews of electronic resources are problematic because, "given the changeable nature of online resources, reviews may no longer reflect the actual product (a full-text periodical database may have added or dropped titles, changed years of back issues, etc.)."[4] In some libraries, the section of reference reviews from some periodicals are photocopied and routed to members of the reference staff for them to recommend titles that should be purchased.

The best sources of reviews for print and electronic reference materials will vary from library to library. Some of the standard print sources are now available online. A few of the print serials that include reviews of reference materials are listed below, with the URLs of their associated websites.

- *American Reference Books Annual* (www.arbaonline.com)
- *Booklist* (www.booklistonline.com)
- *Charleston Advisor* (http://charlestonco.com; online resources only)
- *Choice: Current Reviews for Academic Libraries* (www.cro2.org)
- *Library Journal* (www.libraryjournal.com)
- *Reference & User Services Quarterly* (www.rusq.org)
- *School Library Journal* (www.slj.com)

Many specialized periodicals include book reviews only for specified subjects. Some of these periodicals may be useful to subject specialists who purchase materials for the reference collection and also for those who are developing reference collections for special libraries.

A set of books that may be useful, if a section of the reference collection must be evaluated and/or expanded, is the three-volume set of *The New Walford*. This has been issued, one volume at a time, beginning in 2005. *Volume 1: Science, Technology, and Medicine* was issued in 2005. *Volume 2: Social Sciences* was issued in 2008. *Volume 3: Arts, Humanities, and General Reference* was issued in 2008.[5] Some public and school libraries may find *Recommended Reference Books for Small and Medium-Sized Libraries and Media Centers* to be useful.[6]

Many Internet sites include reviews of print and electronic resources. A list of some of these sites is available at AcqWeb's Directory of Book Reviews on the Web (www.acqweb.org/bookrev.html). Several databases are available that were designed to provide reviews of reference resources. The American Library Association's Guide to Reference (www.guideto reference.org) and ARBAOnline (www.arbaonline.com) are both very useful. The Guide to Reference is the most recent incarnation of a series of classic guides to reference books. Alice Kroeger's *Guide to the Study and Use of Reference Books* was the first edition in the series, published in 1902. Generations of librarians have relied on the successors to this guide, making it such an icon of reference collection development that it was usually referred to only by the editor's last name, the two most recent being Sheehy and Balay.[7]

If the library uses an online vendor database to purchase print and electronic books, the database may offer access to book reviews as an added utility. A common feature of these databases is the ability to set up a scheduled, periodic search for reference books that fit a particular profile. It may be possible to arrange for regularly scheduled e-mail announcements to be sent to members of the reference staff or subject selectors that include records of new reference items for their consideration. An alternative might be for the reference collection manager to review the items in the list, weed out those not appropriate for the collection, and then e-mail the remaining records to members of the reference staff or subject selectors.

Another place to find reviews may be the periodical databases available in the library. Some of these databases may include the full text of the periodicals named above or the full text of other periodicals that include book or database reviews. Many databases permit title or keyword searches to be limited to reviews.

A free source of book reviews might be a library catalog, as some now include reviews for books listed in the catalog. Searching for titles in the catalog of a consortium or large library might yield useful reviews, in addition to being a source of suggested new titles. One way of identifying potential new acquisitions is to check what resources are held by a library that has a good collection in a particular subject area.

General Selection Criteria

Some selection criteria apply to all types of materials that might be considered for the reference collection, although the specifics of these criteria might vary from one type of reference resource to another.

Relevance of content. The first consideration is the relevance of the content to the collection. No matter how much reviewers rave over a book or database, it is worth acquiring only if it fills a need in the reference collection. That doesn't mean that every item acquired for the collection will be one of the most heavily used resources. In general, a selector will look for content that fills a hole in the collection or a title that strengthens or updates the resources that cover a particular subject. A selector might also need to find resources on a subject that is new to the reference collection, responding to curriculum changes at a school or university, altered activities of a company or organization, or new information demands at a public library.

Authority of author, publisher, or database producer. This is particularly important in judging resources that can't be examined before they are purchased. Look for an author with excellent credentials or with a history of authoring well-received reference books. The publisher may be an established, reputable publishing house that is well known for the quality of its reference books on the subject of the potential acquisition. The library may already provide access to databases, produced by a particular organization, that have impressed the reference collection manager or other librarians. Some databases are online versions of print materials that already have an established reputation.

In some cases, it may be the reputation or credentials of the authors of segments of the contents that indicate a certain reputation. For instance, in an academic subject encyclopedia, the individual entries should be signed and the book should include a list of contributors, with the credentials of each author. Another indication of authority in an academic subject encyclopedia is the inclusion of a bibliography of scholarly sources in each entry.

Accuracy. Checking accuracy presents certain difficulties. Frequently, the selector must rely on reviews of the product or on the reputation of the author and/or publisher. If possible, examine the resource before acquiring it, including performing a spot check for accuracy. For example, an examination of a biographical directory of women scientists of the twentieth century might include scanning the lists of entries for scientists who should be part of this type of directory. If the list of entries in this biographical directory included a man, such as horticulturist Liberty Hyde Bailey, it would certainly be cause for concern about the accuracy of the book. Compare several entries with entries in similar reference sources, looking for discrepancies. Check facts that might easily be incorrect, such as birth dates, places and dates of employment, or titles of authored books. The presence of typographical errors might also indicate a lack of attention to detail.

Completeness. This refers both to the completeness with which the book or database covers a particular subject and to the completeness of the individual entries. Different resources are meant to provide different levels of comprehensiveness; each will serve a different audience. A small public library might be quite happy with the level of comprehensiveness offered by a one-volume encyclopedia of psychology, while a research library might be better served by a multivolume psychology encyclopedia. Each of these references is designed to serve a particular type of library user. Some libraries might purchase both, intending each to play a different role in the collection.

Currency. The importance of currency will vary from one type of reference resource to another. A subject encyclopedia that is intended to reflect the state of the art of a topic should include very recent publications in the bibliographies at the end of each entry. An index that is meant to cover the most recent articles should have a very short lag time between publication of an article and the inclusion of it in the database. Some databases that include full-text articles place an embargo on the full text of some issues of the journals and magazines. Many libraries have purchased these databases with the intent that the online full text will replace paper publications. Unfortunately, an embargo can be added to a title or lengthened on an existing title without notice, leaving the library without access to the most recent issues of a valuable title.

Age/user appropriateness. The content and format of the resource must be appropriate to the age and/or reading level of the people who use the library. A librarian in an elementary school library may not wish to purchase a technical, scientific book on dinosaurs, even if the school has many students who are fascinated by dinosaurs. Similarly, if the library serves paleontologists, the reference collection will probably not need a book on dinosaurs that was written for children.

When choosing resources, keep in mind what is appropriate for those who use the library. A public library might purchase a database of information about auto repair that is intended for consumers, while an engineering library might need a database that includes technical resources about engineering automobiles. A public library might purchase a book or database with tax information for consumers, while a library in an accounting firm would purchase tax resources written for tax professionals. Each reference resource is designed for a particular user population, so it's necessary to match the target audience of a resource with the people who use the library. If a library serves more than one kind of user, the reference collection should also reflect this diversity.

A school library or the children's department of a public library may also be concerned about whether content of a resource will be acceptable to the parents of the children who use the library. Resources may need to be checked to see if the language might be considered offensive or if some of the subjects might be objectionable to some parents.

Any library may be concerned with the potential for challenges to books or online resources if some user or user group charges that they are objectionable. The library's main collection development policy will usually refer to the Library Bill of Rights (www.ala.org/ala/issuesadvocacy/intfreedom/librarybill/) or to other documents concerning intellectual freedom, or may include copies of such documents. The library will frequently also have procedures and forms for challenging the appropriateness of library materials. The reference collection development manager should be familiar with these documents and procedures. If there is a challenge to reference resources, the time that was put into writing a reference collection development policy should prove to be time well spent, since one of the purposes of such a policy is to provide a rationale and some guidelines for what materials are to be included in the reference collection.

Accessibility. The intent of a reference collection manager is always to purchase reference materials that will be accessible to all users, but accessibility can be considered in several ways. Frequently the overall collection development policy for a library will include some information about the demographics of the library's user population. Certainly, a discussion with members of the reference staff will result in a profile of those who use reference services in the library.

Many libraries will wish to provide online resources that are accessible to those outside the physical space of the library or the library's parent organization. The license of an online product will define who is eligible to use the resource outside these confines.

A different kind of accessibility may be critical for library users who have some types of disabilities. In order to best serve these users, the library might have a requirement that an online resource work with particular software or offer a text-only version of the user interface and content. Some library users might be helped if the online resource offers the ability to change the size of the typeface or provides other means of making the text more legible. It's long been common for reference desks to provide a magnifying glass for those who wish to consult a reference book that has a small typeface. In fact, the *Compact Oxford English Dictionary* was issued in a slipcase with a magnifying glass. An increasing number of databases with full-text content now provide audio files. A library might have additional considerations that will ensure the accessibility of reference materials to all library users.

Geographic coverage. Because most libraries serve a population in a particular geographic area, reference collections frequently include some types of material that are appropriate for that area. A school library in Pennsylvania might include reference materials that serve students taking a course on the history of the state. A public library in Omaha might provide local business directories. A corporate library might provide reference materials on countries in which the firm does business.

Preferred language(s). The reference collection development policy should include a section on what languages are to be included in the reference collection. A school or university might need to offer language dictionaries or other materials in the languages taught at that institution or in the languages used by students who are not native English-language speakers. A public library that serves a multilingual population might need to provide resources written in various languages. A business or government agency might need to conduct business in multiple languages. In a diverse society, there are many reasons for a library to provide at least some reference sources in a variety of languages.

Illustrations. Whether the source is in print or online, the illustrations should be appropriate to the content, contribute to the reader's understanding of the topic, and be of excellent quality.

Access points in other resources. If the library subscribes to a service such as Reference Universe (http://refuniv.odyssi.com) that provides indexing for a wide variety of reference sources, the presence of a reference source in that database should be considered when choosing materials for the reference collection. If the librarians or library users frequently consult standard bibliographies or other sources that provide access to reference resources, the presence of reference materials in those resources should also be considered.

Cost versus quality. One goal of any collection manager is to acquire those resources that provide excellent value for the amount of money spent. The relative expense of reference resources magnifies the importance of this goal. The reference collection manager must try to predict the potential usefulness of a book or online resource and balance that against the prospective expense. In some cases, the resource may have excellent scope and quality and be very appropriate for the collection, but the price would consume too much of the reference budget or is too expensive for the amount of predicted use it would receive in the library. This doesn't mean that a reference selector should always purchase the cheapest sources. Sometimes the value of a publication is reflected in the higher price, and the more expensive resource might turn out to be the smart choice.

Selection Criteria for Online Resources

Due to the wide variety of online resources, the selection criteria that are used for one title might be quite different from those used for another online title. The criteria used to evaluate an index and abstract database would not be identical to those used to evaluate a database of standards, audio files, or dictionaries. However, there are some criteria that are useful in the selection process for a wide range of online resources.

User interface. Most people prefer a clear, well-organized, clean user interface. The interface should reflect the type of sources in the database and the needs of the target user population. What users desire in an online interface changes over time, which can make an electronic resource whose interface hasn't changed in the previous five years ago appear dated. Online resources should update their user interface as the standards for online graphic design and taste evolve. As new technologies become available, database producers need to incorporate those that will enhance database function and the user experience.

Branding. It's easy for those who use the library's online resources out-side the physical library to forget that they are using library resources. This is particularly true for users who connect directly to the databases they use most often, instead of accessing them through the library website. Many database vendors provide branding opportunities so libraries can incorporate the library name and/or logo into the user interface of the database.

Customization. There may be other ways that a library can customize the user experience of an online resource. If there is more than one search form, many databases offer the ability to choose which of these will be the default interface for all library users. There may be additional features that can be altered, such as changing the name of a button, or choosing which limiters will appear on the search form.

Search features. Many databases offer a basic search form, which is frequently a keyword search shown as a Google-type search box, and an advanced search form. Some databases offer a visual search or other type of specialized search. The program used for processing a search may be a straightforward search of the word(s) in the search box or may be governed by a specialized formula. It should be easy for the user to determine, on the various search interfaces, which search operators are available and how they interact with each other. The available pre- and postlimiters will also vary. Which operators and limiters enhance the searching capabilities of the resource will vary depending on the subject and purpose of the online resource and on what is appropriate for the target audience of the database.

Available indexing. Databases that index articles, books, or other texts typically offer the ability to search at least by keyword, author, and title, but additional search fields will vary. Specialized databases should include index fields that are appropriate to the subject and target audience. A database of photographs might offer a searchable field for primary color of the image or the name of the photographer. A database of children's literature might include search fields for book illustrators, the appropriate age level of readers, literary awards, or lexile range.

Some databases offer a controlled vocabulary in addition to keyword searching. If there is a controlled vocabulary, the precision of terms and presence of a thesaurus should be considerations of the quality of the indexing provided. If the controlled vocabulary uses a standard thesaurus, such as Library of Congress Subject Headings, that should also be noted. Databases such as newspapers that are composed of full-text, digitized historical resources often don't offer a controlled vocabulary.

Linwood DeLong recommends the following questions be asked about journal indexes (and similar questions could be asked about databases that index other formats):

> How thorough is the subject indexing of the journals that are covered by different databases? Are approximately the same number of subject terms applied to an individual article? Is the indexing precise enough to capture the specific topics that are addressed by the article? Is the indexing consistent within the database? Does the database actually index all of the articles that it claims to?[8]

DeLong examined several article databases and found other problems with subject indexing, such as personal names with no birth and death dates, imprecise or ambiguous geographic locations, missing non-English titles, and missing scientific nomenclature. In asserting the importance of controlled vocabulary, he notes that Project Muse "continues to use subject headings to augment the entries for articles because it is essential for reliable and comprehensive user searching, that there be consistent terminology, devoid of inflections or other spelling variations, that is applied consistently, with adequate concern for both broadness and precision, to the articles that are indexed in databases."[9]

Results display. This will also vary by type of resource. In many databases, the result of a search is a list of records for some type of item, such as articles, books, images, or audio files. It should be obvious how these records are organized, whether sorted by author, title, relevance, date of publication, or other factor. It is also very useful to library users to be able to change the sorting method—having the ability to alter the display format is a standard feature and can be quite useful. In many cases, the default display record includes at least a partial citation and may include a portion of the abstract or a portion of the text of the item. Other elements may appear in the display record, depending on the type of material in the database.

Availability of full text. One major consideration in selecting databases of text files is the convenient availability of the full text of indexed items. This might be accomplished by the inclusion of the full text within the database, the ability to link to the full text if it appears in another library-owned database, or, at the very least, the ability to identify library ownership of the title in paper, microform, or another format.

A common method of linking to the full text of an article or book that is in another database is the use of an open URL link resolver. When a database search identifies a particular article or book, the open URL resolver uses the metadata from the record to create a link to the full text that is located in another of the library's databases. The user can then click on the link to be taken to the full text file in the other database. The ability to do this is crucial in order to provide the easy access to full text that is demanded by so many library users. Fortunately, most major database producers market products that are open URL–compliant.

Even when content is available in full text, this designation may not mean that the entire full text is available in the online resource. An online serial may be missing articles, illustrations, even entire issues. An electronic book that is the equivalent of a multivolume print set may not include all volumes or may be missing illustrations, appendixes, or other materials that were present in the print version.

If the database includes full text, the available file may be HTML or PDF full text. The smaller file size of most HTML documents might be preferred by library users who have access only to slow Internet connections, but HTML full text might not include illustrations or indicate page breaks. The larger file size of a PDF file may be much slower to load but provides an image identical to the print version, which is useful for students and scholars who need to format a complete, accurate citation, including page numbers. An increasing number of text databases are offering users the option of listening to an audio file of the text, occasionally even providing voices in a choice of gender or accents. Audio files of full text may be desirable for library users with visual disabilities or for those who may be able to understand spoken English more easily than written English. Sue Polanka writes, "Visualizing information, hearing the pronunciation of a word, or listening to the content in its entirety can be a tremendous help, particularly to those with learning or physical disabilities and ESL learners."[10] Ostergard and Yusko note, "Teen reference could also be improved by providing print reference sources in audio formats . . . Many students today are diagnosed with reading difficulties and simply cannot process information visually. Reference sets with corresponding audio versions would be extremely well received by young adults and the librarians that serve them."[11]

Special features. Database producers offer a very wide variety of special features, depending on the type of items included in the database and the target audience for the product. A database of business articles might allow a search limiter that will identify industry profiles or SWOT analyses. An e-book about animals might include audio or video files that enhance the textual information. Interactive features in some resources include tests that are instantly graded, images that can be edited, games that can be played, and equations that can be used to compute figures.

Ability to save, print, or e-mail results. In many databases, the ability to save and e-mail records or files is critical to users and librarians. Without this capability, the usefulness of a database may be limited for some researchers, particularly if the library charges for printing or restricts printing to only some categories of users. The lack of the ability to print is also a limiting factor in the usefulness of a textual online resource, particularly for users who want to make notes in the margins, highlight important passages, or simply produce a copy to be used at a later time.

Ability to export citations to bibliographic management software. This ability can be a high priority for students and other researchers who use a library that provides access to bibliographic management software. Even if the library doesn't provide the software, this can be a useful feature for students and scholars who use the library.

Updates/currency. Many library users assume that updates to online resources are made almost instantly. Librarians know from experience that this isn't true. Important factors in the currency of a database are the update frequency of content and the lag time between publication date of a title and its appearance in the database. If a database of current newspaper articles is updated even one day late, many library users will not find that acceptable. However, a database of information about animals might not be updated daily, but might be appropriately updated much less frequently. Another factor in currency is the existence of an embargo on some of the full-text titles in the database. If an embargo exists, the database's online title list should clearly indicate the length of any embargo.

The form that updates take for electronic books can vary. If the electronic book was purchased either as a single title or part of an aggregated database, any supplements or new editions may need to be obtained as a separate purchase. In some databases, the library may only have access to an electronic book until the new edition is issued. At that time, the library must purchase the new edition because the previous edition will be deleted from the database. If the book is part of a subscription, the updates and/or new edition may be added to the database. At that time, the previous edition might be deleted or might sometimes be left in the database.

Availability of downloadable MARC records. Some companies offer downloadable MARC records for the individual titles in an aggregated database. Since many library users identify resources using the library catalog, this is likely to increase the use of the database. These records may be included in the price of the database or may be available as a separate purchase.

Having records in the library's catalog for the individual titles within an aggregated database is of primary importance in ensuring that users will be able to discover the resources they need and that the database will receive as much use as possible. It's a waste to spend so much money on online resources if users can't find them. In addition, if members of the library staff don't know what's contained in the library's databases, duplicates may be purchased simply because the selector doesn't realize the library already owns the title.

Usage data. The availability of usage data is an important factor in determining if the library will continue to pay for access to a subscription database. Questions to ask about usage data before deciding to acquire an online resource include: What type of usage data is available for the online resource? How are the available data elements defined? Can a library staff member access the data, or does she have to contact the company to request the desired data? Is the data COUNTER compliant?

Remote access. For many libraries, the ability of users to be able to access an online resource outside the library is crucial. Not all online resources work equally well with all remote-access software programs. In rare cases, resolving problems with remote access may require a series of consultations between the library's computer staff and the technical staff from the database vendor.

Mobile access. Many libraries have begun providing databases that can be accessed by mobile devices such as smartphones, iPods, and iPads and other tablets. Increasingly, library users are asking for mobile-optimized databases, as shown in the results of the California Digital Library survey, which revealed that 53 percent of respondents wanted to be able to search library databases "frequently" or "occasionally."[12] A *Library Journal* survey of academic and public libraries in 2010 found that 54 percent of academic libraries indicated that offering the "ability to access databases" on handheld devices was a priority, after mobile-optimized catalogs, Internet sites, reference services (such as SMS reference), and notices to users.[13]

The California Digital Library survey listed the significant barriers to using mobile devices: screen sizes that were too small, pages that took too long to load, page formats that were difficult to read (such as PDFs), and web page formatting that was difficult to read.[14] If the online resource under consideration offers a version that is optimized for mobile access, this should be tested during the trial period, with particular attention paid to the barriers to mobile use that were revealed in the survey.

When choosing online resources that will be used on a handheld device, it is useful to know what kind of handheld devices will be used by most of the library's users to access databases. For instance, the California Digital Library survey found that the most popular mobile device with Internet capabilities owned by college and university respondents was the iPhone (53 percent), followed by the iPod Touch (20 percent), Blackberry (10 percent) and Droid (9 percent).[15] The mobile version of some online resources is optimized only for a particular brand of smartphone and may not easily be viewed on a feature phone.

Anecdotal evidence suggests that many handheld device users are using their device to identify articles and books for a project, but then reading the full text on their computer. Respondents of the California Digital Library survey reported, "I can't imagine reading a whole science journal on my iPod Touch" and "I tried [to read academic content], like when the professor sends PDFs, but I'm not great at reading it off of the screens." However, this aversion to reading full text on handheld devices wasn't universal. Some respondents who use the Internet on their mobile devices reported that they read books and articles at least daily (26 percent) or weekly (20 percent).[16] The study cited a report from Texas A&M University Libraries about the results of publicizing access to EBSCO mobile databases. They found that only 1 percent of mobile EBSCO users viewed full text that was found as the result of a search, compared with 77 percent who did so when using EBSCO databases on a computer.[17]

Demand for mobile-optimized library resources is likely to grow, although the extent of that demand will differ among libraries. Again, libraries that are considering the acquisition of mobile-optimized online resources should consider carefully what devices are owned by their users, how existing available library resources are being utilized by mobile device users, and how the resource under consideration will fit into the current mobile user experience.

Cost models. Cost models for online resources sometimes seem to be limited only by the inventiveness of database producers and vendors. Acquiring an online resource may be the result of a purchase, a subscription, a lease-to-own arrangement, or a combination of these. If perpetual access of a resource has been purchased, there may also be an annual maintenance fee. The vendor may be able to subdivide the information in a database in various ways, each of which has a different set of prices. The price may be at least partially determined by the full-time equivalent of students at an institution, the number of majors in an academic discipline, the number of residents in a public library district, the number of lawyers and/or paralegals in a firm or office, or any number of other permutations of the potential user group. The price may be influenced by the number of permitted simultaneous users, the number of computers authorized to use the product, the ability of users outside the library or physical location to use the resource, or the requirement that each user have an individual username and password.

There may be some room for negotiation on prices. This is more likely to be true in a poor economy, when there are fewer buyers. At these times, database vendors are more likely to be creative in the deals they offer, and libraries are sometimes more creative in how they fund new acquisitions.

Sue Polanka recommends, "A few ways to save money include buying multiple titles, purchasing through a consortium, negotiating discounts with vendors, and purchasing book titles only *one* time and in one format (e or print)."[18]

Licensing. Online resources usually require licenses. If the library has already acquired at least one online resource from the same company, it might be possible to add the license for the new resource as an addendum to the original license. If the library acquires an online resource through a consortium, the consortium might be responsible for negotiating and administering licensing agreements. In a larger library, a single person might be assigned the responsibility for licensing—perhaps the head of collection development or the head of the library. Because licenses are legal documents, licensing may be the responsibility of an organization's general counsel.

The license will usually define which users are authorized to use the product, availability of remote access, restrictions to the use of the product, and the availability of usage statistics. Some licenses contain terms that are considered to be pretty standard, and there may be little or no negotiation. Other companies include terms in licenses that are problematic; an attorney's advice may be necessary before negotiations are completed. (For more detailed information about licensing, see chapter 5.)

Technical considerations. Some libraries have to take into consideration limitations caused by equipment, software, or networking capability. Usually these problems can be resolved, but they still may require a series of consultations between the library's computer staff and the database vendor's technical department.

Even with well-designed online resources, librarians and library users need to be able to find information about the use and content of the online resource. There should be adequate help pages, online help, and staff training (either in person or through webinars or other online methods).

Not all selection criteria or methods will be equally important to all types of libraries or for every online resource under consideration. In a 2010 ARL survey, more than 20 percent of the respondents rated the following methods of evaluation as "always important":

- Review of the license against the library's existing criteria (46 percent)
- Comparison of content to the library's existing electronic resources (36 percent)
- Ability to work with library systems, such as link resolvers (35 percent)
- Vendor provision of preservation (25 percent)
- Results of a trial (21 percent)[19]

The criteria that are most important will also vary. In the same survey, participants were asked to rate criteria they consider when choosing new electronic resources. "Cost" was the most common deal breaker (38 percent), followed by "compatibility with library systems" (12 percent). A variety of criteria were rated as "very important" by the survey's respondents, the most common being:

- Uniqueness of content (53 percent)
- Relevance to faculty research (46 percent)
- Completeness of content (42 percent)
- User-friendly interface (40 percent)
- Anticipated usage rate (38 percent)
- Cost (33 percent)[20]

Aggregated Databases of Reference Books

Some aggregated databases of reference books offer books only by a particular publisher or by several publishers, while others offer books from a variety of publishers. An aggregated database composed of books from a single publisher makes sense from the point of view of the publisher. Deciding on the boundaries of what will be included in the database is obvious; the publisher doesn't have to negotiate terms with other publishers in order to include certain books; the publisher can design books that will fit well within the database; and the database can serve as a showcase of the books produced by the publisher. However, this kind of aggregated database may not make much sense to the user unless all the books are in a particular subject category, major or minor, such as all humanities, sociology, or social science research methods.

Aggregated databases that include only books from a single publisher or several publishers can also be problematic when developing a reference collection. When a librarian is building a print collection, she rarely collects all the books from publisher A and then the books from publisher B and, if there's money left, she then buys the books from publisher C, and so on. Instead, a print reference collection is built book by book, with the librarian choosing what she hopes will be the best book for this particular collection on subject A and then the best book on subject B, and so on, regardless of which company published each book. In addition, rarely would a reference librarian have purchased all the titles in a publisher-aggregated database. There are almost always some titles that wouldn't have been the first choice for a particular subject. However, because these packages can be expensive, once the budget has been spent on an aggregated database of reference books, the librarian may not be able to afford to also order the books that would have been the first choice for all the subjects included in the database. Many publisher-aggregated databases also include books that cover subjects that wouldn't have been purchased for the reference collection. The same thing would be true if a reference librarian purchased a collection that was composed of all the paper reference books published by a particular publisher. Purchasing aggregated databases that include only the works of a single publisher can result in a collection with less diversity—and one with subject areas for which the library was unable to purchase the most appropriate resources because there wasn't sufficient funding left over.

However, there are also advantages to aggregated databases. If the cost of the database is considerably less than the total cost of the individual items in the database, the library can achieve substantial cost savings, assuming the library would have purchased many of the titles in the database. Also, using an aggregated database provides the user with a consistent experience for multiple titles.

In 2002, Adam Hodgkin—then with xrefer.com, which became Credo Reference—listed some of the advantages of aggregated databases of reference books:

1. By combining reference works together at one URL, the reference service becomes much better known to potential users and easier to find.

2. By tackling a number of reference works, there are economies of scale in production and development.

3. The user's search session is likely to be much more powerful and fruitful, since a collection of reference resources "behind" a common interface can be meta-searched. By firing a search term at the "collection of books," the user finds hits across the whole library, and this is a procedure impossibly time-consuming with any modest collection of printed books.[21]

Given these advantages and disadvantages of aggregated databases, what strategies might be used to choose the best databases of reference books? Sue Polanka recommends librarians "focus on content, select an interface, and negotiate prices. First, libraries should investigate the titles and collections available from all vendors and choose content that fits the needs of the library, not the needs of the publisher's package. Pick and choose titles that will get used, and don't purchase titles twice—with so many publishers and products, it can be easy to duplicate."[22]

Selection Criteria for Free Internet Resources

Ideally, librarians would use substantially the same criteria for free Internet resources as for all online resources, but in practice many librarians loosen these criteria if the resource is free. In fact, there are some criteria that obviously can't be used. These would include:

Branding. There are few free Internet sources that can be branded with the library's name, address, and/or logo as can commonly be done with online resources that must be purchased.

Customization. Similarly, few free Internet sources can be customized to make them more useful for the library and its users. There are exceptions, such as PubMed (www.ncbi.nlm.nih.gov/pubmed/) that offer some level of customization.

Availability of MARC Records. Few free Internet resources provide downloadable MARC records for full-text items. However, many libraries catalog Internet sites. Occasionally a library will catalog all of the individual items within an Internet site. One example of this type of valuable project is the Kent State University Libraries' project to catalog the documents from the Hathi Trust Digital Library (www.hathitrust.org) and Project Gutenberg (www.gutenberg.org/wiki/) and upload these records to the Kent State University Libraries catalog (http://kentlink.kent.edu) and the OhioLINK Central Catalog (http://olc1.ohiolink.edu/search/).[23]

Usage data. It's very unusual to find a free resource that makes any usage data available.

Remote access. This isn't a consideration, as free Internet resources are available to all. Free Internet resources can be particularly valuable for use in chat, IM, or e-mail reference transactions—the reference librarian doesn't need to be concerned about whether the person asking the question has access to the resource being recommended. Because of this, it can be helpful to include links on the library's list of available databases to some free Internet sites for databases such as ERIC (http://www.eric.ed.gov), PubMed (www.ncbi.nlm.nih.gov/pubmed/), Agricola (http://agricola.nal .usda.gov), or Worldcat.org (www.worldcat.org), even if the library subscribes to another version of these databases.

Cost models. Obviously, free sources won't have cost models, although there are some free resources that are also available as subscription databases.

Licensing. This is also not usually an issue for free resources, although some web resources publish the terms and conditions for using the site.

Technical considerations. If something goes wrong with the access to a free Internet site, the library can attempt to contact the producer of the site. However, there's no guarantee that any assistance, or even an answer, will be forthcoming.

The main problem with using free Internet sites for reference work is deciding where to set the boundaries for this part of the collection. Assuming reference Internet sites are organized in some formal scheme, it can be very difficult to define which free resources should be included and even more difficult to determine what should not be included. Anybody who doubts the existence of many truly valuable Internet sites need only look at the sources listed on sites such as the Internet Public Library (www. ipl.org), the Library of Congress's Virtual Reference Shelf (www.loc.gov/ rr/askalib/virtualref.html), or the annual MARS Best Free Reference Web Sites. This annual list has been produced by the Emerging Technologies in Reference Section of the American Library Association's Reference and User Services Association since 1999. At the section's site (www.ala.org/ ala/mgrps/divs/rusa/sections/mars/), there are links to the current list, an archive of previous lists, and an index to previous lists.

Selection Criteria for Print Monographs

For many years, the assumption was that a reference monograph would be published as a paper book in one or more volumes and organized in a recognizable fashion, and that there would be a table of contents and/ or one or more indexes to provide access to the individual entries within the book. Because librarians and most library users have a certain degree of familiarity with using books, most librarians think of books as easy to use. However, not all reference books are created with the same degree of usability. Here are some of the things to consider when selecting print reference monographs.

Physical features. Reference books should have binding that will withstand the normal wear and tear of being handled by a number of people. This normal wear and tear should include the ability to be placed on a scanner or photocopier without causing the binding to crack. Some reference books, such as directories or travel guides, are likely to be useful only for a few years, so the durability of the binding may not be as important a consideration as it would be for some reference books, such as a poetry encyclopedia, a dictionary of first names, or an encyclopedia of the American Revolution, which should be useful for many years. The durability of the binding is more important for this type of reference book, which is expected to have a long shelf life. Oversized books are more likely to need rebinding because they are so often shelved on their spines, causing greater pressure on the binding. Thick books tend to have problems with the binding cracking, and therefore they may need to be rebound more often. Paperbound books that are heavily used or that have a long shelf life may also need to be rebound. Any rebinding adds to the cost of the book, and if the text was printed with an inadequate inner margin, the book might be difficult to read after being rebound.

The quality of the paper may be an important factor for a book that is expected to have a long shelf life because the pages might become brittle and fall out. Poor quality paper can also prevent a book from being rebound, limiting its shelf life.

Visual qualities. Images in all books should be of good quality and large enough to be easily seen. The illustrations should be appropriate for the type of reference book and the intended audience. Although there are reference books in which illustrations are appropriately printed in black-and-white, in many cases color illustrations would be desirable, if not mandatory.

The typeface should be easily read. Some books are published in a very small typeface in order to save money, but this is not a savings if library users are unable to read the book.

Ease of use. Some books have excellent content but have not been well organized, so that it is difficult to find information when needed. It should be easy to determine how a book has been organized, and the scheme of organization should make sense for the subject covered. The table of contents and indexes should be easy to find and use, and should provide access to the particular features that will make the book most usable. The index should use terms that are appropriate for the subject and the intended users of the volume. In a multivolume set, the index should direct the reader not only to a page number, but also to a specific volume so that the reader doesn't have to guess which volume will have the desired entry.

Updates/currency. Some monographs are updated with supplements or yearbooks. If these are necessary, the librarian may wish to place a standing order or subscription to ensure that the library receives all updates. If a publication requires regular updates, the timing of the updates should reflect the relative urgency of the need to be updated. Transmittal sheets for legal or tax materials are generally time sensitive, so they should be received soon after being issued. An annual weather almanac should be received from the supplier soon after publication because library users may wish to consult it as soon as they see a media announcement that the new edition has been published. If a particular reference resource must be kept current, many libraries will choose to receive that title online, with the expectation that an online version will be more current than a paper version.

If possible, before purchasing a new edition of a reference book, it should be checked to determine if the new edition contains sufficient new information to justify the expense, or if the new edition is substantially the same as the previous edition, except for the inclusion of a new introduction.

Cost models. Of course, books may be purchased when on sale to save money. The library may be able to purchase books at a discount by using a company that offers a certain percentage discount for quantity. The library may be able to obtain a discount by purchasing through a consortium. Updates or books in series may sometimes be purchased at a lower price by setting up a standing order or subscription. Occasionally, access to the online version is included in the price of a print book, although that access may be for only a limited time.

Selection Criteria for Print Serials

Reference serials include a variety of materials, such as:

- Books that are updated with transmittal sheets or pocket parts
- Books that are sometimes updated with one volume of a multivolume set becoming two volumes
- Publications issued at regular intervals (annually, monthly, etc.)
- Publications issued at irregular intervals (multivolume sets issued over an extended time period or publications replaced at irregular intervals)
- Multivolume sets that combine two or more of these types of serial publications

Physical features. Whether the type and quality of the binding and paper is a factor may depend on the type of serial. If a book is updated with transmittal sheets or pocket parts, the main volume may be kept on the shelf for a long time, and only the updated portions will change. In this case, it is important for the binding and paper of the main volume to be durable. If the updates are frequently replaced, it may be acceptable for them to be published on less durable paper and have cheaper binding.

If publications are issued at intervals, the importance of the binding quality will depend on how long the volumes are expected to be used. If new volumes replace older volumes, and the older volumes are discarded, it may be acceptable to have cheaper, less durable binding and paper. If paperback volumes are kept, they may need to be rebound, which adds to the cost of the resource. In addition, if they are rebound, the quality of the paper may be more important so the paper doesn't become brittle, causing pages to crack and fall out.

Ease of use. As a reference source grows to include more volumes, the organization and points of access become more critical. Whether a serial is updated with transmittal sheets, pocket parts, or added volumes, the indexing must also be updated to reflect the added pages in order for the newer information to be discoverable. In some cases, a multivolume set that is issued one volume at a time may not have any indexing until all volumes have been issued. If this set replaces an earlier edition, it may be necessary to keep the entire earlier edition until the complete new edition, including indexes, has been received. In some cases, it may be possible to use the index for the earlier edition to determine approximately where the updated information might be found in the new edition. If the new edition has been substantially reorganized, some entries may prove extremely difficult to find until the new indexes have been issued.

Print indexes are generally issued as either one-step indexes, in which the indexing and citations are in a single list, or as two-step indexes, in which the indexing is contained in a separate section and refers to the records in the abstract section. One step indexes may also provide additional points of access, in the form of secondary indexes to the records included in the main part of the index. For instance, a periodical index might be organized by subject, but it might also include supplementary indexes for elements such as author, or article titles, or for particular types of entries, such as book or film reviews. Two-step indexes frequently provide multiple types of indexing that all refer to the records in the main part of the index. In the case of the two-step index, one common problem is that the user must page back and forth between the index and the abstract in the same volume, or between an index in one volume and the abstracts in a different volume.

Updates. Many reference serials are, by definition, the mechanism by which a title is kept current. When considering update cycles of reference serials, the issue is most likely to be whether the information contained is as current as needed for the particular subject covered in the resource. A practical consideration is the amount of time needed to file the updates. If a title is kept current by means of weekly transmittal sheets that must be filed, it might be a good candidate for replacement with an online resource.

Cost models. Reference serials are generally purchased either as a subscription or a standing order. Subscriptions are usually a one-time annual expense. This is most used for titles issued on a regular basis, so that a specific number of issues can be expected in a particular time period. Standing orders are frequently used when the number of items received in a specified time will vary. The library is generally billed for standing orders as publications are received. This can make it difficult to budget for standing orders; the number of items received can only be estimated, and therefore the amount to budget can only be estimated.

Examples of items that might be received as standing orders are:

- Volumes of a multivolume encyclopedia, issued irregularly
- Pocket parts for a major legal set
- A directory that is issued every two to five years
- An atlas that is updated only after there have been sufficient changes

Cost versus quality. Because serial publications are ongoing expenses, the librarian must balance the usefulness of the title against the expense. Theoretically, this should be no more important than in any acquisition. However, serials budgets tend to increase and can easily absorb substantial portions of the total reference budget. Not only does the price of a serial publication frequently increase each year, but the serial arrives automatically. It's easy to forget about individual serial titles, particularly if the library pays for reference serials out of a general serials budget instead of having a separate reference serials budget. It's very important to regularly review the reference serials that are being received to be sure they are still fulfilling the purpose for which they were originally selected. In addition, as more databases are added, some of these serials may be included in an online resource, resulting in the library paying twice for the same content.

NOTES

1. Alice Bertha Kroeger, *Guide to the Study and Use of Reference Books: A Manual for Librarians, Teachers, and Students,* Boston: Houghton, Mifflin & Co., 1902, vii.
2. Kay Ann Cassell and Uma Hiremath, *Reference and Information Services in the 21st Century: An Introduction* (New York: Neal-Schuman, 2006), 289.
3. Doug Johnson, "Managing the Intangible: Digital Resources in School Libraries," *Library Media Connection,* August/September 2007, 47.
4. Ibid.
5. Ray Lester, editor-in-chief, *The New Walford: Guide to Reference Resources, Volume 1: Science, Technology and Medicine,* (London: Facet, 2005); Ray Lester, editor-in-chief, *The New Walford: Guide to Reference Resources, Volume 2: Social Sciences* (London: Facet, 2008); Ray Lester, ed., *The New Walford: Guide to Reference Resources, Volume 3: Arts, Humanities, and General Reference* (London: Facet, 2008).
6. Shannon Graff Hysell, *Recommended Reference Books for Small and Medium-Sized Libraries and Media Centers* (Littleton, CO: Libraries Unlimited, annual).
7. Kroeger, *Guide to the Study and Use of Reference Books.* Other recent editions include: Eugene P. Sheehy, *Guide to Reference Books* 10th ed. (Chicago: American Library Association, 1986); Robert Balay, ed., *Guide to Reference Books* 11th ed. (Chicago: American Library Association, 1996).
8. Linwood DeLong, "Subscribing to Databases: How Important Is Depth and Quality of Indexing?" *The Acquisitions Librarian* 19 (2007): 100.
9. Ibid., 101–105.
10. Sue Polanka, "Interactive Online Reference," *Booklist,* Jan. 1 and 15, 2010, 116.
11. Maren Ostergard and Shauna Yusko, "What's Missing in Reference Collections for Young Adults," *Booklist,* Sept. 1, 2006, 172.
12. Rachael Hu and Alison Meier, *Mobile Strategy Report: Mobile Device User Research,* 2010, 27.

13. Lisa Carlucci Thomas, "Gone Mobile," *Library Journal*, Oct. 15, 2010, 31.
14. Hu and Meier, p. 22.
15. Ibid., p. 20.
16. Ibid. p. 25–26.
17. Ibid., p. 27.
18. Sue Polanka, "Options for the E-reference Collection," *Booklist*, Nov. 1, 2007, 84.
19. Richard Bleiler and Jill Livingston, *Evaluating E-resources*, SPEC Kit 316 (Washington, DC: Association of Research Libraries, 2010), p. 52.
20. Ibid., p. 47.
21. Adam Hodgkin, "Integrated and Aggregated Reference Services: The Automation of Drudgery," *D-Lib Magazine* 8 (April 2002). doi: 10.1045/april2002-hodgkin.
22. Polanka, "Options for the E-reference Collection," 84.
23. Kent State University Libraries. *University 2010 Fall Report: Collections*, www.library.kent.edu/page/16055.

FOR FURTHER INFORMATION

Leonhardt, Thomas W., ed. *Handbook of Electronic and Digital Acquisitions.* New York: Haworth Press, 2006.

Safford, Barbara Ripp. *Guide to Reference Materials for School Library Media Centers*, 6th ed. Santa Barbara: Libraries Unlimited, 2010.

Yu, Holly, and Scott Breivold. *Electronic Resource Management in Libraries: Research and Practice.* Hershey, PA: Information Science Reference, 2008.

5

Acquisitions, Budgets, and Licenses

EXCEPT IN A small library, a reference collection manager is usually not responsible for maintaining control of the materials budget and ordering materials for the entire collection. However, it is important to understand how these functions are performed in the library, in order to be able to manage the money that is allocated for the reference collection. One way of achieving this understanding is to meet with those who are responsible for these operations—to see how they perform their tasks and to learn the rules of how these systems work in the library. The people who work in budgets and acquisition can be instrumental in teaching a reference collection manager how to work effectively within the procedures of the library.

Acquisitions

The acquisitions process consists of ordering resources and ensuring they are processed so they can be cataloged and made ready for use. Each library will have its own policies and procedures, and one of the responsibilities of the reference collection manager is to learn and follow the acquisitions policies and procedures. The people who work in acquisitions will be the best source for learning these policies and procedures.

In some libraries, the person who selects materials for the reference department may need to do the ordering, to type out paper or online forms for each item and send these to the appropriate publisher or vendor. More typically, the selecting and ordering will be done by someone ordering via a vendor's database. Acquisitions will place orders for selected items. The reference collection manager might also have the authority to go to a bookstore, publisher, or vendor and purchase items using a credit card or other credit line.

Except in small libraries, the reference collection manager will probably need to give requests for reference sources to the acquisitions staff, which will do the actual ordering. This might be done on paper but will more likely be accomplished online.

Once the item has been ordered, the reference selector may not need to do anything else until the item arrives and is ready to be added to the collection. With a print item, this may mean that it arrives in the reference office to be put on a shelf of new reference books so the reference staff is aware of new items; or it may mean that the new item is placed in the reference collection. When an online resource is purchased, there is also usually a procedure to be followed that includes cataloging, branding and customizing the user interface, ensuring remote access, adding it to the list of available online resources, and doing other activities that prepare an online resource for use.

In most libraries, the integrated library system (ILS) includes an acquisitions system that is part of the integrated library system's management, but some reference collection managers prefer to keep a separate list of the items that have been requested so these titles can be tracked as they travel through the acquisition system. This can be done using spreadsheets or even simply making a list of titles and whatever additional information is desired. An advantage of using spreadsheets is the ability to reorganize the data as needed. An option that results in lists of the titles that have been requested—an option that requires little time or effort—is to print out the list of orders as they are placed, although this series of lists would include only the information available when the title was ordered. Information for monographs that might prove useful would be author, title, publisher, date of publication, date requested, date acquisitions placed the order, anticipated price, date arrived, actual price, and date received in reference department. This type of data collecting is time consuming, and not all reference collection managers find the results to be worth the time spent, unless the library's ILS system does not include an acquisitions system or the library does not have an ILS.

Because many online resources are acquired as databases that aggregate numerous titles, purchasing online resources may result in a list of acquisitions that includes fewer individual titles. However, because of licensing and technical issues, acquiring an online resource can sometimes take months of negotiations and consultations. It's easy to forget what's already been accomplished and what still needs to be done in processing each new online resource, particularly as there are frequently a number of people involved in this process. It helps to keep a file on each online resource or to have a checklist that reflects the various steps in the process followed by the library. If there's a librarian or library user impatiently waiting for a particular database, this provides a way to track the progress so they can be reassured that the resource is being processed so it will be ready for use. Because of the complex nature of online acquisitions, an increasing number of larger libraries have instituted the position of electronic resources librarian to better organize and manage this process.

Inevitably, there will be an occasional book that needs to be returned. A vendor should always accept the return of any damaged book. This might include a book that was incorrectly manufactured, such as a book that was bound upside down or one with pages missing. A book might also have been damaged in handling or shipping. A vendor should accept the return even if the book has been marked with a property stamp or spine label. Sometimes a book has been firm ordered, and the book has perhaps already been stamped and labeled. At this point, the selector changes his mind and decides the book does not fit into the reference collection. Can the library return such a book? The practical action to take is to check the vendor's policy for returns. However, there's also an ethical side to this question. Is it ethical to return a book to the vendor, after making it unsalable, when the library has firm ordered the book? Linda Brown, chair of Bowling Green State University's Collections and Technical Services Department, argues that this is not an ethical practice. If the library has firm ordered a book and processed it, preventing it from being sold to another library, the library has an obligation to pay for the book and not return it.[1]

Some reference books may be received through a library approval plan. An approval plan is negotiated between the library and a vendor and defines a group of books and/or order slips for books that will be sent to the library. As part of the approval plan a library may receive books, order slips for books, or both. The approval budget lines may be allocated by subject area, or there may be a single budget line for all approval books. If the library's approval plan involves the vendor shipping books to the library, these books are commonly placed on shelves for selectors to review, although some libraries will automatically add all approval books to the collection. If approval-plan books are placed on shelves to be reviewed by the selectors, the reference collection manager should form the habit of quickly reviewing all the approval books to discover if there are books that ought to be in the reference collection but have been designated for the main collection. Depending on the agreement with the vendor, the books may even arrive shelf-ready, with much of the processing already done. If books arrive shelf-ready, they can't be returned to the vendor. If reference books are received as part of an approval plan, the books received must be periodically evaluated so the plan can be revised if needs have changed, if there are gaps in the plan profile, or if the titles sent are consistently unwanted. A normal level of returns for approval plans is 2 to 4 percent. If more than 8 percent of books received are designated to be returned, it might be time to evaluate the reference portion of the approval plan. If only order slips are sent to the library, selectors will have an opportunity to choose which books will be ordered, but no books will be automatically shipped.

Budgets

As Linda Brown, Bowling Green State University's chair of Collections and Technical Services, explains, "A library's budget reflects the library's collection development policies and goals—what the library sees as important." She notes that "money talks" and is the better indicator of what the library's policy goals are for the collection than what is written in the library's collection development plan. However, she also says that a library's budgetary goals may change from year to year.[2] For instance, a university library might temporarily spend an increased amount of money on a particular subject due to the addition of a new academic program. A public library situated in an area that has experienced layoffs might allocate a greater proportion of the budget to purchase books and online resources on topics such as job hunting, home and car repair, vegetable gardening, and personal money management.

Even when there is no need to allocate some of the budget for a special purpose, there never seems to be enough money to acquire all the reference materials that would be useful for any library and its users. Learning how the budgeting process works in the library can make it easier to use the available money to the greatest effect.

The structure of budgets will vary from library to library. In some libraries there isn't even a separate budget line for reference. This can create a situation in which reference materials—particularly expensive ones—are sometimes not purchased in favor of purchasing less-expensive materials for the general collection. If there are no budget lines allocated for reference, but instead all are allocated for subject areas and controlled by subject bibliographers, interdisciplinary or multidisciplinary reference materials may not be purchased because individual subject bibliographers may not want to commit a substantial portion of their budget for materials that are tangential to their subject area. In addition, reference collections sometimes cover subject areas not included in any subject bibliographer's particular discipline.

In most libraries, however, there will be a separate budget line or perhaps more than one budget line for reference. Some libraries will have a single budget line that must cover all reference materials. There may be several budget lines, defined by format. For instance, there may be separate budget lines for print, microform, and electronic resources. The budget lines may be defined by whether the materials purchased are monographs or serials. The reference collections manager may not control every one of these budget lines. In some libraries, the reference collection manager may only be able to request that materials be acquired from one or more of these budget lines that are controlled by the head of collections, the director of the library, or some other person.

In addition to budget lines that are designated specifically for the acquisition of reference materials, there may be other budget lines from which some reference materials may be acquired, such as approval plan budget lines, funds for replacement copies, or funds resulting from grants. In addition to a budget line for reference databases, or instead of that budget line, there may be a general database budget line for the entire library. The reference collection manager may be able to request that items be purchased from these budget lines that are controlled by somebody else. In some institutions there may be the opportunity to convince another office or department outside the library to fund all or part of a resource. This is more likely to be possible if a resource is primarily used by that office or department and if it is quite expensive.

Before beginning to order materials, a new reference collection manager should investigate what budget lines can be used to acquire reference collection resources and who controls each of these budget lines. Although it's useful to know if there are other budget lines that might be used for reference materials but are controlled by somebody else, it's important to begin by working with the budget lines designated for reference. Few people who control other budget lines will be willing to use their own budget lines to purchase reference materials if the money in the reference budget lines isn't being spent.

Once the reference collection manager knows what budget lines are available, the next step is to discover how much money is in each of these budget lines. In many libraries, at the beginning of the fiscal year the materials budget will be allocated, and each person who manages a budget line will be told the amount of money available in each budget line. It's important to keep track of how much has been spent and how much money is left. There may be a deadline by which the money should be spent, although this is more common with budget lines meant for the purchase of monographs. There may be a series of deadlines, each indicating a date by which a certain percentage of the budget line should be spent. At the end of the fiscal year, the unspent money may be rolled over to the following fiscal year, used for special end-of-the-year purchases, or used to purchase other resources.

How much information must be kept on each budget line will vary from one library to another, or vary by the level of detail preferred by an individual budget manager. If the library uses a computerized system to keep track of budgets, a budget manager might feel comfortable relying on the data in that system to perform this function. At the very least, a reference collection manager should know how much money is still available in each budget line she controls. Useful budgetary amounts to know are how much money was in the budget line at the beginning of the budgetary period, how much is encumbered (what the library has promised to pay), how much has already been paid, how much is left to spend after encumbrances are subtracted, and how much is left to spend after the amount paid is subtracted. This information is generally included in the ILS, but the currency of the information may vary. This information may be automatically added to the ILS when the order is placed. If, however, the information must be manually added to the ILS by the acquisitions staff, the information in the system may be slightly out of date. If the reference collection manager doesn't have access to up-to-date financial data, the acquisitions staff should be able to provide this information.

Notice that there are two separate ways of looking at the amount of money that's been spent or encumbered and, therefore, of what remains to be spent. The first way is to look at how much has been encumbered. When materials are ordered, the amount the library expects to pay for the item is entered as being encumbered because the library has promised to pay this amount. However, that amount can change as circumstances change. The price of an item may change before it arrives. The price may be less or more because it was on sale, because the publisher or distributer has discounted it, because the price has increased or decreased, or because shipping charges were added or were greater than anticipated (if the amount of shipping was included in the encumbrance). The item that was requested may have been discontinued or be out of stock. The publisher may have decided to not publish this resource. In these cases, the amount the library had expected to spend should be subtracted from the amount that was encumbered. The amount that is encumbered for an item and the amount that's left to spend after encumbrances can fluctuate until the bill for the item has been paid or until the acquisitions staff knows the item won't be arriving.

The second way of looking at what's been used from the budget line causes budget lines to change in only one direction. As payment is made for the items that have been acquired, the line of the budget that shows how much has been spent goes up and the line that shows how much money is left to spend goes down.

The amount that can safely be spent is the amount that hasn't been encumbered because that amount of money hasn't been spent and also hasn't been promised to a publisher or distributor. Just remember that the amount of money that's encumbered and the amount that is available to be spent will change as circumstances change. It's not usually necessary to keep track of the changes in the price of individual items as the price goes up and down and as the books arrive or are canceled. The acquisitions staff will take care of that. But, it is necessary to check how much is left after encumbrances in order to know how much money is left to spend in a budget line.

It's fairly easy to keep some control over expenditures in budget lines for items that must be ordered, such as monographs. Controlling overspending in budget lines for continuing expenses is more difficult because these materials will automatically continue to arrive unless they are canceled before they arrive. Some of the budget lines for continuing expenses that might be available for reference materials are database, serials, and standing order budget lines.

Most databases are billed annually, although it is sometimes possible to schedule the invoicing for some other interval. In some cases, the library can negotiate a lower price by paying several years in advance. If a database provider normally schedules all billing on a fiscal or calendar year schedule and the library wishes to gain immediate access to the database, the first invoice may cover part of a year or a year plus a segment of another year so that the next invoice will cover the standard fiscal or calendar year. In general, the price of most databases will increase each year. Typically, the library will need to cancel an online resource well before the payment is due. This time period should be defined in the license agreement. A typical license agreement might define this time period as thirty days, but a license might specify another time period, such as ninety days. It's good practice to produce a list of the databases to which the reference department subscribes and the date by which a renewal decision must be made so these decisions are made in a timely fashion and the library is not obligated to pay for a database because a cancellation deadline was missed.

Serials are also usually billed annually. These also need to be canceled before the receipt of materials or access. Serials subscriptions may be examined individually before the invoice is expected to arrive, or a list of all reference serials may be produced and the entire list reviewed at the same time. The list of which subscriptions to cancel will then be given to the acquisitions or serials department, depending on the normal practice in the library. The important thing to remember is that when subscriptions are canceled, the money saved is often not available until the following fiscal year because it may have already been spent from the current year's budget line.

Standing orders are usually not billed on an annual basis, because this budget is reserved for items that arrive irregularly. Therefore, the amount allocated to that budget line is usually based on an estimate of how many items will be received in a given year. Typical items that are purchased from a standing order budget line are pocket parts that supplement legal publications, transmittal sheets that replace individual pages in tax publications, or volumes of a multivolume set received on an irregular schedule. Not only may the number of volumes published each year vary, but they may be received as they are issued, and not in sequential order. The library will typically be billed when the items are shipped to the library. It is difficult to anticipate how much money will be needed in a standing order budget line in any given year because the number of items received will vary for any particular title. Standing orders will typically be billed and paid for as they are received, unlike serials, which are usually billed before they are received. Thus it may be possible to cancel a standing order at any time during the year, canceling future shipments.

One of the difficulties of controlling all types of serials budgets is that prices for individual titles generally rise. If the amount in the budget line doesn't increase by at least the same amount as the collective price increase, some of the serials must be canceled or money will need to be added to that budget line, perhaps by moving money from another of the reference budget lines. The temptation, at a time when many libraries are purchasing fewer print monographs, is to transfer money from that budget line. Although this solves an immediate budget problem, it can also be a very quick way of reducing the monograph budget line. Moving money from monograph to serials budget lines should be carefully considered to ensure that this action reflects the planned development of the reference collection. This practice of transferring money from monograph budget lines to serials budget lines has been accelerated in many libraries by the increasing number of paper titles that have been replaced by online serials subscriptions.

Because serials titles usually need to be canceled prior to the renewal date, it may not be possible to reduce the amount spent from the serials budget lines for the current budgetary year if it becomes apparent that price increases will result in an overspent budget line. It may be necessary to request that the acquisitions staff move money among the budget lines controlled by the reference collection manager to solve the problem for the current year. This should be combined with evaluating the titles that are purchased from the affected serials budget lines in order to cancel sufficient titles so that the problem is not likely to recur during the following budget year.

Of course, this assumes the reference collection manager will have the authority to move money among reference budget lines, that he can convince the person with the authority to do so, or that he can convince another budget manager to transfer some money into the reference serials budget lines. Each library's budget system works differently, so each reference collection manager will have to investigate the options available in the library and adjust his budget strategy accordingly.

Licenses

Most of the licenses required for reference products are for electronic resources. The terms and conditions of these licenses are negotiable. Libraries need to carefully review and evaluate licenses to make certain that the terms permit the institution to use the content in ways that will meet their institution's and community's needs; to ensure that their institution's best interest is not compromised; and to make certain that the library and parent institution can abide by the terms and conditions. Finally, if the institution is bound by state law, the license must comply with that law. Governing law and indemnification of the licensor by the licensee are frequent clauses that need to be modified or struck for a state-supported institution to comply with state law. Frequently, licenses are reviewed by the institution's legal counsel as well as by a librarian.

Because reference collections frequently include many online resources, it can be very time consuming to negotiate and manage these licenses. The number of licenses to be managed might be lessened by purchasing online resources through a consortium, since the consortium will frequently negotiate the license on behalf of all members of the consortium. If the library has previously acquired online resources from the database provider, the new products may be added as an addendum to the original license. If both the library and vendor have signed onto SERU, the Shared Electronic Resource Understanding, that NISO standard may replace the electronic resource license (www.niso.org/workrooms/seru/).

Some companies post a copy of their license, or terms and conditions, online, so it can be evaluated before the library makes a decision to acquire a particular product. In other cases, the license must be requested from the database vendor. A few examples of licenses, or terms and conditions, are posted online, including:

> JSTOR Terms and Conditions (www.jstor.org/page/info/about/
> policies/terms.jsp)
>
> OCLC WorldCat.org Terms and Conditions (www.oclc.org/worldcat/
> policies/terms/)

In most libraries, the person who selects reference materials is not the person who negotiates licenses. Instead, this responsibility may lie with the head of collection development, acquisitions or serials librarians, or an electronic resources librarian. Especially in a small library, the library director will have the responsibility for reviewing and negotiating licenses. The responsible librarian may also need to consult the institution's counsel before finalizing a license agreement. One of the reasons responsibility for negotiating licenses is generally assigned to one individual is that a license is a legal contract between the company that grants the license and the library.

Although the reference collection manager will probably not need to be the library's expert on licenses, it is helpful to have a general familiarity with the content of license agreements. Doris Van Kampen cautions, "The goal of your database provider will be to define the rights as narrowly as possible so that the maximum amount of revenue can be obtained. The goal of the library should be to define the license as broadly as possible in order to increase the leverage of the library's budget and to protect the patron's right to free access to information."[3] The reference librarian needs to make certain that the library's license negotiator is aware of the reference department's use of and needs for an electronic resource. Some resources may have restrictive clauses for printing or downloading content, or for placing content in an electronic reserve system or a campus content management system. If the reference department has specific concerns about use of the content, those needs must be communicated to the license negotiator.

Not all libraries will rate the components of licenses equally, but a survey of ARL libraries found that the two licensing terms that were most likely to be deal breakers were applicable law (25 percent) and walk-in users (20 percent). The most common licensing terms that were considered to be very important were:

- Interlibrary loan (42 percent)
- Electronic reserves (40 percent)
- Walk-in users (38 percent)
- Cancellation restrictions (31 percent)[4]

The following sections are frequently found in licenses:

Definitions. This section may define some of the terms in the licensing agreement. Lesley Ellen Harris argues that certain terms should be defined because they can "define the parameter of the license." Terms that she believes should be defined include:

- Commercial use
- Content (being licensed)
- Interlibrary loan
- Licensed content
- Premises
- Territory

- Not for profit
- Noncommercial
- Educational use
- Authorized uses
- Authorized users[5]

Names of both parties to the agreement. This will include the name of the company (the licensor) and the name of the library or institution (the licensee) signing the agreement.

Name and URL of the material being licensed. This may include the name of a database or of a segment of a database. If a library is acquiring a part of a larger database, this section should reflect precisely the segment that will be licensed by the library.

Authorized users. This should specify who is allowed to use the online resource. For a public library, this might include library employees, walk-in users, library card holders, or users who live within a particular geographic area. For schools, it might include employees of the institution and currently enrolled students. For colleges and universities, it would include both of these categories of users, plus visiting scholars and walk-in users. It might also include students who are enrolled at branch campuses—or those locations might have to negotiate separate license agreements. In rare cases, colleges and universities might list off-campus alumni as authorized users in the license. A survey in 2005–2006 found only 18 of 102 university libraries offered such access.[6] For government offices and other organizations, authorized users might include employees of the institution, temporary workers, and possibly walk-in users.

Remote access. This clause should specify that all authenticated, authorized users may access the resources regardless of physical location. Occasionally, licenses may specify restrictions for where those users are located. In some cases, databases can be used only within the institution or only within the library. Most licenses forbid the library to share databases with other institutions.

Permitted uses. This section details how the licensed content may be used and may cover the following:

- Printing, saving, or downloading materials
- Interlibrary loan
- Electronic reserves
- Use of materials in course packs
- Posting of content or links to content in a campus course management system
- Sharing articles with colleagues
- Posting of content or links on Internet sites, blogs, etc.
- Use of MARC records that are received from the database vendor

Privacy or confidentiality. This section lists what, if any, data about individual users is collected and how that data can be used by the company.

It may also specify whether the terms negotiated with the individual institution are confidential. Some libraries are now objecting to the inclusion of these nondisclosure agreements, or NDAs. In 2011, Cornell University, a private university, posted a document on its website that stated, "To promote openness and fairness among libraries licensing scholarly resources, Cornell University Library will not enter into vendor contracts that require nondisclosure of pricing information or other information that does not constitute a trade secret."[7] Some public universities were already unable to enter into contracts that included NDAs because of state sunshine laws. Cornell had been forced to drop one license because the publisher refused to remove the nondisclosure clause, and instead the university purchased the print edition.[8]

Price and payment. This includes the cost of the product and the terms of the payment. It also includes the notification requirement for cancellation, which is typically anywhere between thirty and ninety days prior to the renewal date.

Terms and conditions. This clause lists the time period for which the library has access to this online product. This may be a term between specified dates, or the library may have purchased perpetual access. If the library has purchased perpetual access, the license agreement should be specific about what this means. The contract should list the necessary conditions for terminating the library's contract with the database producer. It should also detail the conditions that would cause the database producer to terminate the contract with the library. For instance, a database producer might be allowed to cancel a library's access to the database if the library didn't abide by the license provisions that define authorized users. The license should allow for a period for the party that breached the license to cure the problem. This cure period should be mutual, providing both licensor and licensee an opportunity to remedy a breach.

The library's liability. Database vendors might expect a library to make certain efforts to ensure their users are abiding by the conditions of the contract that affect their use.

Indemnification or limited liability. This clause should state the limits of the liability that are incurred by each party in connection with this database. Some states prohibit a state institution from indemnifying another party. If this is the case, any indemnification clause that requires the licensee to indemnify the licensor should be struck from the contract. if the licensing library is part of a state institution.

Governing law. This section stipulates what state's or country's laws govern the terms and conditions of the contract. Most libraries want a license to be governed by the laws of the state or country in which the library is located.

Usage statistics. This specifies what usage statistics are available and how this data will be made available to the library. It should say if the data is COUNTER compliant (www.projectcounter.org). COUNTER (Counting Online Usage of NeTwork Electronic Resources)–compliant data is standardized so that it's easier to compare usage data between several online resources. The database vendor may also be compliant with the SUSHI standard to allow COUNTER-compliant usage data to pass electronically from the vendor's SUSHI-compliant system to the library's SUSHI-compliant electronic resources management system. SUSHI is the Standardized Usage Statistics Harvesting Initiative (www.niso.org/workrooms/sushi/).

NOTES

1. Linda Brown, private communication to author, Feb. 26, 2011.
2. Ibid.
3. Doris Van Kampen, "Acquisitions and Copyright," in *Handbook of Electronic and Digital Acquisitions*, ed. Thomas W. Leonhardt (New York: Haworth Press, 2006), 3.
4. Richard Bleiler and Jill Livingston, *Evaluating E-resources*, SPEC Kit 316 (Washington, DC: Association of Research Libraries, 2010), 49–50.
5. Lesley Ellen Harris, "Taking Time to Define Terms in License Agreements," *The CRIV Sheet*, February 2009, 10.
6. Catherine Wells, "Alumni Access to Research Databases: The Time Is Now," *College & Research Libraries News*, July/August 2006, 414.
7. Cornell University Library. "Nondisclosure Clauses," www.library.cornell .edu/aboutus/nondisclosure/ (accessed Sept. 27, 2011).
8. Jennifer Howard, "Cornell U. Library Takes a Stand with Journal Vendors: Prices Will Be Made Public," *Chronicle of Higher Education*, March 21, 2011, http://chronicle.com/article/Cornell-U-Library-Takes-a/126852/.

FOR FURTHER INFORMATION

Albitz, Becky. *Licensing and Managing Electronic Resources*. Oxford, England: Chandos Publishing, 2008.

Chandler, Adam, and Tim Jewell. "The Standardized Usage Statistics Harvesting Initiative (SUSHI)." *Serials* 19 (March 2006): 68–70.

Copyrightlaws.com (blog). www.copyrightlaws.com.

Harris, Lesley Ellen. *Licensing Digital Content: A Practical Guide for Librarians*. 2d ed. (Chicago: American Library Association, 2009).

Liblicense. "Licensing Digital Information: A Resource for Librarians." www .library.yale.edu/~llicense/.

Shepherd, Peter T., and Hazel Woodward. "The COUNTER Code of Practice for Books and Reference Works—A Primer," *Serials* 22 (November 2009 Supplement): S39–S44.

Yu, Holly, and Scott Breivold. *Electronic Resource Management in Libraries: Research and Practice* (Hershey, PA: Information Science Reference, 2008).

6

Collection Maintenance

REFERENCE COLLECTIONS, BOTH print and electronic, require constant and time-consuming maintenance. This comes as no surprise to any member of the library staff, although people outside the library sometimes assume that if it's online, it just takes care of itself. Instead, those involved in the maintenance of a reference collection frequently find that many small tasks add up to a significant workload. This doesn't mean that all the collection maintenance will be performed by the reference collection manager, but it must be done by somebody. In a large library, this responsibility will typically be shared by a number of people, each of whom has a specific role to play. This chapter covers some of the typical collection maintenance functions and duties.

Maintenance of New Electronic Resources

Just as each new reference book must be placed in the most appropriate place in the print collection, each new electronic resource must be placed in a virtual location so it can be discovered and used. If the library catalog is the primary means of discovering electronic resources, this might mean simply cataloging the resource. If the library produces a list of electronic resources, this new one must be added to the list. Information in a record for an electronic resource might need to include a description of the content, types and dates of materials covered, relevant terms of the license, available tutorials or help files, access information, ability to access remotely, availability on mobile devices, availability of contents for interlibrary loan, and any additional information that might assist the user to access the database. The new resource may need to be added to subject guides or other resources that the library provides to assist users in identifying useful library resources. Listing the new resource in an appropriate manner is only one of the maintenance functions that must be performed for each new electronic resource.

A new electronic resource should be tested on the most common types of operating systems, browsers, and equipment on which it is likely to be used. If the resource will be available remotely, it will need to be tested outside the library or institution, preferably on several computer/browser/Internet service company configurations. If the online resource offers an interface for mobile devices, this should be tested on the most commonly used types of handheld devices. The resource should be tested with the library's link resolver, bibliographic management system, discovery layer, or other software. Because there are so many factors that influence the way in which electronic resources perform, there's never any guarantee that it will work in all situations, no matter how carefully it is tested, but testing the most likely combinations will reduce the number of complaints from library users. Many technical problems that arise during testing will be solved by the library's information technology staff, but there will sometimes need to be consultations between the library's information technology staff and the technical staff of the database vendor before all apparent technical problems are solved.

Increasingly, there are administrative functions involved in the management of the user interface or other components of an electronic resource. Many databases provide branding opportunities for adding library logos, headers, or other indications that the database is made available by a particular library or institution. Links may need to be added that provide access to the library's link resolver, interlibrary loan software, or ask-a-librarian service. Many online resources permit a certain amount of customization, such as whether the default home page will be the basic search or the advanced search, which limiters will be available, or what wording will be used on certain buttons or links. For instance, the library may be able to choose whether to use the term *scholarly journals*, *academic journals*, or *peer-reviewed journals* as a search limiter. A good practice is to establish the library's preferred terms and then to follow that whenever the database administration protocols will allow. It's easier for library users to understand the choices available to them when terms are consistent.

If the database includes full-text content such as articles, books, music, videos, audio files, or maps, some of these individual items may need to be cataloged. In some cases, the database provider makes available downloadable MARC files for the individual items in a full-text database. Cataloging individual items from an aggregated database will sometimes dramatically increase the use of the database.

If the new electronic resource replaces a print reference source, a decision must be made about what should be done with the resource that's being replaced. The print resource might be kept on the reference shelves. If the library owns a series of print volumes that are being continued by online resources, some libraries place a label on the book(s), or a book dummy on the shelf, indicating that newer information is available online. If the print resource is removed from the reference collection, a book dummy or sign at the location of the print resource could indicate online availability. The older print materials might be left in the reference collection for a period of time, with the intention of making a final decision about disposition sometime in the future. If this is the case, determine a deadline and put a note in the calendar or tickler file as a reminder that this decision must be made. If the reference collection manager conducts a continuous review of the print reference collection, this decision could be deferred until the next time that portion of the print collection is reviewed.

Library staff and other interested parties should be notified when the new resource is available for use. It used to be that the addition of a new electronic resource was frequently followed by a time period for library staff to learn the new resource. During this time there was frequently an in-house training session conducted either by a representative of the database provider or vendor, or by a member of the library staff. Rarely does a library now allow time for the library staff to learn a new electronic resource. There may still be staff training sessions available from the database producer or vendor, but now these are more likely to be provided as webinars or other online tutorials instead of in-person sessions.

Maintenance of Existing Electronic Resources

An amazing amount of time must be spent to maintain the library's electronic resources. Because the successful use of electronic resources is dependent on the intersection of the database software, the operating systems on each piece of equipment involved, the browsers used, data networks, etc., there are many things that can go wrong—not all of them under the control of the library.

Each change to the user interface or structure of a database may be the catalyst for a series of technical changes that must be made to ensure that the database is still accessible and functional for the library's users. As the user interface and organization of the electronic resource changes, the listed URLs for the resource as a whole or for certain segments of the resources used by the library will need to be changed, perhaps in multiple places. Any tutorials or help files produced by the library may need to be revised.

Branding and customization may need to be changed. Remote access software and link resolvers may need to be tweaked. Directions for exporting citations to bibliographic management software may need to be revised.

While the library subscribes to an online resource, the usage data should be collected periodically to determine whether the library should continue to subscribe to the title. If this data is stored for future use, it will make collating such data much easier when a decision about retention of the title must be made.

If the content changes, cataloging records may need to be added or deleted. If individual journals or books from an aggregated database are included on any list maintained by the library, the lists may need to be revised. If the library has canceled journals or other resources because the title was available in a particular database and the journal is removed from that database, the library may need to subscribe to the paper journal or find another online source for the content. In a database that aggregates full-text content, the titles included can change without notice, so the reference collection manager and other library staff members may not immediately realize that important content has disappeared from the library collection.

In addition to losing access to individual titles within an aggregated database, a library sometimes loses access to an entire electronic resource. Some of the reasons this might happen include the company neglecting to send a bill to the library, the library neglecting to pay a bill on time, the library's name accidentally being dropped from the list of subscribers at the company, the company deciding to discontinue a product, the company ceasing operations, or any one of a series of technical difficulties that might cause a disruption in service. In some cases, nobody seems to know just why the library's access was dropped. However, whenever access to an online resource ceases, somebody needs to determine what caused the problem and then find a way to fix it.

There are so many things that can go wrong with a collection of electronic resources that some libraries have created the position of electronic resources librarian. Whoever is responsible for maintaining the smooth working of the online reference collection needs to keep in communication with other members of the library staff, IT staff, and people who work for the companies responsible for the production and dissemination of the electronic resources. Maintaining control of the library's electronic resources can sometimes seem a little bit like trying to hold on to a greased pig!

Maintenance of New Books

Reference books should already be cataloged and labeled before they arrive in the reference department but may need to have additional labels added.

Some libraries use colored dots, labels, tape, or other methods of designating that a book is meant to be shelved on index shelves, a dictionary stand, an atlas stand, the ready reference shelves, or another designated place. Labels or stamps may need to be added to remind staff and users that the book is not allowed to circulate or may circulate only for a limited time. If the book is shelved in a special location, there may need to be a book dummy placed in the main reference collection to direct users to this location.

When a book is placed in the reference collection, a decision must be made about the disposition of any earlier editions or volumes. If the library has a general policy on how many editions of a reference book should be retained, this should be noted in the reference collection development policy. If this decision is made title by title, this should be noted in the staff mode of the catalog record for the title. If there is no way for the reference collection manager to note this in the ILS or catalog, there may need to be some other file that will compile this type of information so that a new decision doesn't need to be made each time a new edition or issue of a book arrives. This can be accomplished by including the information on a spreadsheet or word processing file, or in a card file. Keeping a record of these decisions is more important than the format in which they're kept. Any format can be used that is convenient to access, update, and maintain. The format chosen should also be capable of being easily transferred to the next person in charge of the reference collection to access, update, and maintain.

Most reference collections contain many serial publications. Reference serials are as complicated—and sometimes as frustrating—as serials in other parts of the library. It's no coincidence that some of the earliest reference resources to be converted to online format were indexes and abstracts. Reference serials can be published on a regular schedule, such as annual, quarterly, or monthly publications, but they might also be published on an irregular schedule, such as transmittal sheets or pocket parts that arrive only when there's a change to a particular part of a publication. A record should be kept of which parts need to be kept for each title. For instance, the record would indicate if semiannual volumes replace monthly issues, or new pocket parts replace old pocket parts. The person who shelves the new volumes should have access to these records, or a note could be placed on the new item indicating what should be done with the old volume. Shelving transmittal sheets, pocket parts, and other updates can take a significant amount of time. As part of this process of filing updates and new volumes, older materials may need to be transferred to another collection or withdrawn.

As new monographs are shelved, the shelver should try to notice if there is an older edition of the monograph. If older editions are routinely removed from the reference collection, this should be done when the new edition is added to the shelf.

As new books are placed on shelves, some shelves will become too full and some shifting may need to be done to make room for the new books. This can be a particular problem with some reference serials unless older volumes are removed to make room for the new volumes. In fact, this is sometimes the impetus for weeding a portion of the reference collection.

Some libraries like to place new reference books on a new books shelf or include them in a list of new books to ensure that interested parties are aware of the new resource.

Maintenance of Existing Print Collections

While a print resource is part of the reference collection, it may need to be reshelved and, as part of that process, have the use recorded. In some integrated library systems or catalogs, this may be easily done by recording the bar code or other identifier of the book in a system that will aggregate the data for use by the library staff. In some libraries there may be some other type of database or file in which use is recorded. Other libraries stamp the date, write a check mark, place a colored dot, or make some other indication on the book to note that the volume needed to be reshelved and therefore must have been used.

Library staff members who handle a reference book should try to notice the physical condition of the book. Hardbound books may need to be rebound, have pages glued back in, or have pages replaced. If oversized books are shelved on their spines, it isn't uncommon for the spines to crack. Books that have been bound so they're very thick are also more prone to have broken spines. Paperbound reference books may also need to be rebound. Sometimes pages will separate from the spine and need to be reattached. Paperbound books can also be more difficult to keep upright on a shelf, particularly if they are not very thick. In this case, the volumes might need to be placed in a magazine file or some other container in order to keep the shelves neat, facilitate shelving, and prevent damage to books. The label on any reference book can become faded over time and need to be replaced.

Inevitably, as additional books are added to the collection, some shelves will get too full. These shelves can be weeded or the books can be shifted to make the collection easier to use. As sections are shifted or weeded, a good practice is to put the books in correct order so that users will more easily be able to find the book they want.

Although it is a common practice to rearrange the order of books while shelving, it is also useful to read the shelves. This is a job frequently given to new reference staff in the hope that, in addition to restoring the collection to the correct order, it will help them become familiar with the contents of the reference collection and with the classification system used in the collection. Other goals of reading a collection might be to identify missing volumes in multivolume sets, to discover earlier editions of reference books that should be removed from the collection, to identify books that are in poor condition, to find nonreference books that have been shelved in the reference collection, and to find books that have been shoved behind the rows of books. In some libraries the books are also edged—that is, the spines of the books are moved to line up with the front edge of the shelf.

A time-consuming but useful practice is taking an inventory of the reference collection. The first step is to make a list of books in the order in which they should be shelved. This is simplest if the library still has a card shelf list. Simply take the card file into the shelves and check the cards or list against the books on the shelf, noting what is missing. However, it is the rare library that still has a card shelf list. Many integrated library systems or catalogs can be used to make a list of reference books in call number order. This list can be printed out or displayed on a laptop, notebook, or handheld device. The list of books can be checked against the books on the shelf. The method used for noting missing or damaged items will vary by the method used to make the list. This process is generally faster when participants work in teams of two: one person checks the list while the other checks the books on the shelf. Although this can be a tiresome and tedious job, it is an effective method to identify missing and damaged books, put the books back in order, and gain a greater knowledge of the content of the collection.

Routine stack maintenance is also necessary. As books are added and removed, some books may need to be shifted to make room for new books or to even out the spacing of the books on the shelves. Major future shifting projects can be avoided, or at least delayed, if some space is left on each shelf to allow for growth. This practice also makes it easier to remove the books on the shelf, which lessens the likelihood of damage to the binding of the books. When books are packed tightly on a shelf, users frequently remove them by pulling on the top of the spine, which sometimes breaks the top edge of the binding. Other routine stack maintenance tasks include adding bookends to keep books from falling over, removing bookends as shelves become too full, moving shelf labels, or changing the labels on the ends of the shelves. There may be other tasks that need to be performed to keep the shelves neat, with the goal of making the collection as easy to use as possible.

Marketing New Reference Resources

New reference sources might be marketed to library staff or to library users. It's important for reference staff—and sometimes other members of the library staff—to know what new materials are available and how these can be used. In some cases, new reference materials might be marketed to library users or potential library users. The library might want to market some new reference titles to a very general audience of library users or might target specific groups of library users who are more likely to be interested in a title.

The easiest way of informing reference staff of new resources is to place the books on a new books shelf for reference materials, located near the reference desk. If members of the reference staff make a habit of regularly checking this shelf, it can be an effective method of keeping up to date with the new print acquisitions. If the library has an online list of new books, new reference books might be included in the list of all new books or might be on a list that includes only new reference books. Other ways of marketing new reference resources might include creating book displays, writing articles for library newsletters or institutional in-house publications, sending e-mails to targeted groups of users, placing announcements on bulletin boards in the library or elsewhere within the organization, putting notices on library blogs or Twitter accounts, placing flyers or table tents in the library or elsewhere in the organization, addressing departmental meetings outside the library, sending notices to community organizations, including information about new resources in class or workshop sessions, or listing new resources in online or print resource guides.

Marketing doesn't have to be used only for new resources. Some of these same ideas could be used to increase the use of older resources or underused portions of the reference collection.

The Print Reference Collection as a Physical Entity

Unless the reference collection is totally virtual, it exists in a physical space and needs to be viewed as a physical entity. It's easy to walk through the reference area every day and not really look at that area unless there's a particular reason to look at it, such as planning where to put additional computers, considering whether to initiate an information commons, or making some other change to the use of space in or near the reference area.

In many libraries, the reference area occupies some of the most prime real estate in the library, so it's important to make the best use of the space. Try to imagine what the reference area would look like if it were completely empty. Think about how it is used and what the best design would be if there were no restrictions on how to configure that space. How much of that space should be used for a print collection? How should it be arranged? Should there still be specialized collections within the reference collection, such as a ready reference collection, an atlas or dictionary stand, or index shelves? Which materials should be in the closest proximity to the reference desk? After imagining what the perfect reference collection would look like, compare that to the way it currently looks. Think about how often those books are used, how many times there are people in the aisles, and how many reference books typically need to be reshelved.

Look at the disposition of the books on the shelves. Are most of the shelves full? Is there room for growth? What kind of shelving would best suit the way the reference collection is used? What would be the ideal height for the shelving? Do some library users have difficulty using the books that are on the bottom or top shelves? It can be difficult to read the labels on the books that are on the bottom shelf, particularly for those with bifocals. Removing books from the top shelf may be dangerous, or impossible, for short people, those using canes or walkers, or those in wheelchairs. Is there sufficient space between ranges so the books are accessible to people in a wheelchair or using a walker or cane? Are there adequate spaces within the collection for users to place an open reference book? This is particularly important when consulting large, thick, heavy books. Because so many reference books fit this description, some users may find it uncomfortable to stand and hold the larger books long enough to find the information they want. An easy solution is to leave some shelves empty at a convenient height to hold books that are in use. If there is sufficient room, some tables or counters could be interspersed between ranges or placed at the end of some ranges.

It's not uncommon for a reference collection to grow too large for the amount of use it gets. Logically, as users and librarians rely more on online reference resources, the print collection should be reduced in size, but that doesn't always happen. A serious review of the print collection can result in a reduced number of volumes. Even if the number of shelves doesn't change, this can be an opportunity to remove the books from the top or bottom shelf, or to empty some shelves that could be used to hold books while in use.

Also look at the labeling in the shelving area in general. Are there adequate and accurate labels on the end of the ranges and, if necessary, on the shelves so users can find the desired book? If some reference books are shelved somewhere other than in the main reference collection, is this clearly marked? Are there labels on the special locations within the reference area, such as ready reference collections, index shelves, atlas stands, and dictionary stands? Can users easily determine that a particular title is shelved in one of these alternative locations? This can be done with book dummies or shelf labels, or the library might rely on locations marked in the catalog record for the title.

It can be difficult to stand back and look at the reference collection as if it were the very first time. If there's a new reference department employee, ask her to look at the collection and make suggestions for improvement. Ask her what she particularly likes about the reference collection in other libraries she's worked in or used. Other ways to find good ideas for improving the look of the reference collection could be to visit other libraries, or look at pictures of reference areas on the Internet or in print sources. After taking a fresh look at the reference area, think about what actions could be taken to improve it and the reference collection within the budgetary and time constraints that exist. A collection that looks attractive and current is more likely to be used by both librarians and library users.

7

Weeding the Reference Collection

WEEDING MAY SOMETIMES be called *reviewing* or *deselecting*. Maria Isabel Fernandes defines it: "'Weeding' is the process of removing materials from the collection. It is the process by which librarians control the overall health of a collection."[1] Some librarians make a distinction between weeding and reviewing. They define reviewing to include a more comprehensive examination of the collection, which should discover missing or damaged materials, determine parts of the collection that have grown outdated, and identify areas of the collection that need to be expanded. Reviewing the collection may also include examining lists of serials and standing orders that can be canceled before they are received, with the goal of preventing unwanted materials from arriving and then needing to be weeded.

Most of the literature on weeding collections concerns the print collection. However, this process is just as crucial for the electronic reference collection. In fact, many libraries have electronic books in the reference collection that are now out of date and should be weeded. In addition, it is necessary to review the collection to see that it contains the resources that will serve the needs of reference staff and library users.

Why Are Some Librarians Reluctant to Weed?

Many librarians find it difficult to weed the print reference collection, even when it's rarely used and has become more of a legacy collection. In many cases, there is a similar reluctance to perform a systematic review of the electronic collection, although there's less written about this. This reluctance to weed is one of the reasons so many print reference collections become bloated, making it difficult to find the books that will answer a particular reference question. A collection can easily get into a cycle where the collection looks old and dingy, causing people to be unwilling to use it and also causing it to be difficult to use, which then causes it to look even older and dingier, etc.

What are some of the reasons people give for not weeding?

- I'm just too busy.
- I don't know how to weed.
- I don't know enough about this subject to be able to weed.
- It's not a high priority.
- It's a tedious, time-consuming job.
- It doesn't feel right to discard a book that looks new.
- The book is a standard source or classic.
- Ten years ago I used that book all the time.
- If a book looks old it's because it was used, so we should keep it.
- Just because a book is old doesn't mean it doesn't still have value.
- If I remove a book, somebody might complain because they wanted to use it.
- Somebody else in the library consortium might need it.
- It needs to be in reference to keep it safe.
- I don't want to put it in a collection where it will circulate.
- All the other books in this series are in reference.
- The book got great reviews.
- It was a very expensive set of books.
- Weeding creates a lot of work for people in other departments and they're busy.
- If I discard books, the administrator will think I'm wasteful and will lower my budget.
- Weeding will be controversial for the library's administration.
- Weeding can become a public relations problem.

Why Weed the Collection?

In most collections of physical items, some items become old, damaged, outdated, or unneeded, or have other qualities that make it desirable to remove them. Most people see a need to go through their clothes periodically to remove those that have holes, missing buttons, or stains, or are simply out of fashion. Similarly, people sort through the items in a refrigerator to cull food that is past its use-by date or is no longer appetizing. Weeding a collection of reference books serves a similar purpose.

Some libraries have carried out studies to determine how much of the print reference collection is being used. In 2003–2004, librarians at Stetson University analyzed use of the print reference collection during the four busiest months of the academic year and found that 8.5 percent of volumes and 9.7 percent of titles of their print reference collection were used.[2]

In 2006–2007, librarians at the Winter Park (Florida) Public Library performed a similar study and found that only 13 percent of the volumes and 19 percent of the titles were used in a year. They decided "a substantial number of reference books are not used. One might even conclude that they are not as integral to a functioning reference collection as one would like to believe" and asked, "Can a 1.0 collection survive in a 2.0 world?"[3]

In 2007, Jeannie Colson reported on the results of a five-year use study done at Columbia International University. They placed colored dots inside the back cover of any reference book that had to be reshelved. Over the five years, only 29 percent of the print collection was heavily or moderately used, and 35 percent was never reshelved at any time throughout the entire study period.[4]

What are some of the reasons to review and/or weed a print collection?

- To make room for newer books
- To remove unneeded materials
- To remove out-of-date materials
- To improve the appearance of the collection, encouraging people to use it
- To discover materials that have been shelved incorrectly
- To identify missing materials so they can be replaced, if desired
- To rediscover useful reference books that have been totally forgotten
- To identify subject areas that should be expanded or updated
- To identify subject areas that should be downsized or eliminated
- To discover damaged books so they can be withdrawn, repaired, or replaced
- To replace shelves of reference books with computers, group study spaces, etc.
- To downsize a collection before it is moved, bar-coded, relabeled, etc.

Similar reasons exist for reviewing an electronic collection. Just as materials in the print collection become unneeded or out of date, so do the materials in the electronic collection. Because the library usually owns the materials that are in the print collection, the staff may feel empowered to deal with an outdated, legacy collection. It's much more difficult to control electronic resources, which are frequently not owned by the library, but only licensed.

Baumbach and Miller sum up why weeding is necessary: "Because your students deserve the best collection you can offer them. Less is more. Discard the items that need to go and you'll have more space, more 'curb appeal,' and more accurate, more relevant, more appropriate resources."[5]

Determining the Ground Rules

Before planning the weeding project, the ground rules must be set. Everybody who's going to participate in the project should understand why the weeding project is necessary, what goals have been set, and what role each person will play in the project.

If the need is primarily to downsize the collection, the criteria for weeding may be different than if the main goal is to make the collection more current. This is also the time to decide if the entire collection will be reviewed or only a portion of the collection. If the main goal is to downsize the collection in the least amount of time possible, one solution would be to review only the larger multivolume sets because weeding these would gain the greatest amount of shelf space for the least amount of work. If the goal is to free up space in tight areas, the plan might be to weed only those areas, leaving the less congested shelves for another time. If the major goal is to make an old, out-of-date collection more current, an effective method might be to start by reviewing books published before a particular date. However, if the plan is to do a comprehensive review, a title-by-title review of the collection is the best solution.

Everybody involved must understand his or her role in the project. This includes not only the people who will be doing the actual weeding, but also those in other departments. A weeding project will create work for people in technical services, access services, storage facilities, or other departments within the library or in the library's parent organization. It's important to be considerate of the people who work in these departments and verify they will be able to accommodate this disruption to their normal workflow. This is crucial if the weeding project will be done in a short amount of time, sending hundreds or thousands of books to other departments for processing.

The criteria for removing books from the reference collection will need to be determined. These criteria will vary depending on the goals for the review, but common reasons for weeding a book include:

- Lack of use
- Availability in another format
- Lack of presence on standard lists of recommended sources

- Comprehensiveness of information
- Duplication of information in other sources
- Lack of citations to reference sources
- Age of materials
- Availability of newer edition(s)
- Number of copies available
- Condition of book
- Usefulness for circulating collection
- Language of book

Lack of use is not always easy to determine. The integrated library system may have at least some of this data if it's used to keep track of what books are reshelved or if reference books are allowed to circulate. In some libraries, a mark is placed in or on the book every time the book is reshelved. Some libraries keep very complete records of the sources used by reference librarians to answer questions. Whatever the method of indicating use, this data will probably not completely reflect the use of the item because some library users reshelve volumes, even when there are signs asking them not to do so. Books may be more likely to be reshelved if there aren't adequate spaces within the stacks to place a book while it's being used. Certain types of books may be more likely to be reshelved; for example, books in a large, multivolume set, such as an index.

Usually, if the book is available in an additional format, it is available online. Some libraries have a policy that reference books will be removed from the reference collection if they are also available online. Before removing a book due to online availability, it might be wise to make sure that the entire content of the book is available online. Sometimes the database vendor has decided not to include certain sections or features of the print book, such as appendixes, images, graphs, or tables.

Some libraries use the presence of reference books on standard lists of recommended sources as one of the criteria when deciding if a book should be weeded. If this is the case the standard lists must be chosen and copies placed in a convenient location for use by the reviewers. These standard lists of sources will vary considerably by type of library but will often correspond to sources that were used as selection aids.

Reviewers may evaluate the level of comprehensiveness of the book and the degree to which that information is duplicated in other titles. This is most necessary when comparing similar titles, particularly if the subject area must be downsized.

Some reference books include inadequate citations to sources. Encyclopedia articles may neglect to provide complete citations to the sources that are listed for additional research, or may neglect to provide any sources for research. Some quotation books may give only the author's name as a source for a quotation, with no more exact citation.

Books are often candidates for weeding because of their age. This may not indicate the book is older than a designated number of years but rather that the information is not up to date or is no longer accurate. Unless the reference collection is composed only of a single subject, there will probably be no firm rule that all books published before a particular date should be weeded. Instead, the concept of age will vary with the shelf life of the book. A family medical guide or legal handbook might be current enough for only a few years, while an encyclopedia of ancient China or a dictionary of Greek and Roman mythology might be useful for quite some time.

Some libraries keep only the most current edition of a reference book in the collection. However, the policy might be to keep multiple editions of some kinds of reference books, such as statistical compendiums, yearbooks, almanacs, and indexes.

The policy may be to keep only one copy of most reference books, but some libraries might find it useful to keep multiple copies of certain kinds of reference books, such as style guides, thesauruses, dictionaries, or other heavily used titles.

A book that is in very poor condition might be replaced or sent to the bindery. Poor condition might be an indicator of age, and the book might be removed because it is out of date. On the other hand, a book that is more than five years old and still in pristine condition might be removed from the collection because its condition is an indicator that it isn't being used.

Some books might be weeded because they are receiving little use in reference, but might be useful in the circulating collection. This type of book will vary from library to library, but some libraries might choose to move travel guides, bibliographies, pocket foreign language dictionaries, books on single authors, books on games, or other categories of books to the circulating collection.

The languages included in a reference collection will vary, depending on the user population, the purpose of the collection, and the degree of usefulness of the materials. A library might shelve only English- and Spanish-language books in the reference collection because the user population includes people who read these languages. A library might also choose to keep only certain types of foreign language books in the reference collection. For instance, a library might choose to keep general foreign language dictionaries in the reference collection because they are well used, but move specialized subject foreign language dictionaries, such as a Spanish-English business dictionary, to the circulating collection because they are rarely used.

The books that are kept in the various specialized collections within the reference collection also need to be weeded. It's easy to forget these titles because they sit in separate shelving, stands, or cabinets and can easily become part of the furniture, remaining almost hidden in plain sight. One of the collections that frequently needs weeding is the ready reference collection. This collection is designed to be a repository for books that are heavily used at the reference desk. As new books are added to the shelves, books that are no longer heavily used may continue to sit, unused and unnoticed. This collection can be weeded as part of a more comprehensive weeding project or as a special project.

Librarians from Mankato State University decided to weed their extensive *ready reference* collection because "librarians had insinuated their favorite titles, books that required a long walk to retrieve, heavily used items, books prone to theft, or *reference* materials on little-known topics into this collection." They redefined *ready reference* to include six areas: "special tools of the library trade, basic compendia, major sources to answer frequently asked questions, up-to-date directories, indexes to frequently sought information, and security for heavily used *reference* works."[6]

The Virginia Commonwealth University's library solved a similar problem by moving all but a few titles into the general reference collection. As librarians found that some of these titles were still used, they replaced them on the ready reference shelves and reduced the 210 titles to only 34.[7]

If the library is a U.S. government depository, any books that were received as depository items and are going to be withdrawn should be referred to the librarian in charge of the U.S. government depository collection. She may want the documents returned to the depository collection. If the items are still to be withdrawn, this must be done in compliance with Title 44 of the U.S. Code, the regulations of the U.S. Government Printing Office, and those of the appropriate regional depository. The depository librarian will be able to ensure that this is done.

Another potential complication of weeding applies to members of a library consortium. Some consortia have a policy that the last copy of a book within the consortium should be retained. If this is the case, books recommended for withdrawal should be checked against the holdings of other consortium members to be certain they should not be retained as a final consortium copy.

Planning the Review

In a one-person reference department, or in a larger department where the expectation is that the reference collection manager will perform a one-person review, the planning will be less complicated than at an institution where many people will be involved. The time necessary to plan a weeding project is frequently proportional to the number of people who will be involved.

Mosher delineates the steps in planning a review of a collection:

- Determine the amount of staff time needed and available from all affected library departments.
- Write procedures and design any necessary forms.
- Develop a project timetable.
- Inform participating staff of the goals and procedures, the timetable, and weeding assignments.
- Consult with faculty on the plan itself and on the disposition of materials to be removed from the collection.[8]

Some of the questions that need to be answered during the planning phase include:

- Who will be the project manager?
- Who will assign the areas to be weeded?
- Who will be involved in the weeding?
- Will other people outside the reference staff be consulted in weeding decisions?
- Who will review the materials that individual reviewers have recommended for removal?
- If there is a dispute, who will arbitrate?
- What will be done with materials that have been removed from the collection?
- What will the time line be for the project?

The planning and administration of a collection review project will be smoother and less time consuming if it is done by a single person. In a larger library where more people are involved, a priority of the project manager will be to communicate effectively with those involved in the project, the library administration, and other people who are not directly involved but have concerns about the project.

Weeding the Book Collection as a Major Project

Although weeding the collection as a major project is sometimes called *crisis weeding*, this may be the most practical way to weed some collections. Librarians may be unable to conduct a continuous weeding project due to time constraints. For instance, a busy school librarian might have available only one or two weeks before the school year begins or after the school year ends to do this type of project. This may also be the most practical way to reduce the size of a reference collection when it must be done in a short amount of time.

When the collection is large and the time frame is short, there will need to be many hours devoted to the project. One person, no matter how hardworking, would not be able to weed the entire collection. Usually, many or all members of a reference staff will be reviewers for this type of project. If the collection development staff is separate from the reference staff, it's possible they will also be reviewers. Determining which librarians will be reviewers may depend upon who selects the books for the reference collection, whether this project is a priority for the library as a whole, or how much time has been allotted for the project. The advantage of having the collection development staff involved is that this group should include subject specialists whose knowledge will be valuable in making decisions about what books are most important in particular subject areas. However, the reference staff is most familiar with what materials are needed for reference transactions. The ideal situation would be to assign the subject specialists from reference and collection development to review the section of shelves that correspond to their subject expertise. This may not be practical; most libraries will not have subject specialists for every subject represented in the reference collection. In addition, the number of shelves devoted to books on each subject area will not be comparable. Some reviewers could be assigned much larger sections of books to review than other reviewers—a situation that can disrupt a project time line and cause some participants to feel that they are being asked to do a disproportionately large share of the work. Few librarians think of weeding as a fun task. Assigning uneven weeding sections isn't likely to improve people's attitudes.

The first step in dividing up the shelves that must be reviewed is to count how many shelves of books are in the reference collection. In order to end up with assigned areas of shelving that appear to be fair, it's necessary to allow for differences in shelf counts that are caused by very large multivolume sets. Count the total number of shelves (after making adjustments) and divide it by the number of people doing the review. This will give an approximate number of shelves to assign to each person, although there may be valid reasons for assigning a larger or smaller than average number of shelves to some participants. A common goal is to match participants' subject expertise or interest with the subject areas of the reference collection. Certainly this is desirable in order to have the person with the greatest subject knowledge be responsible for choosing what should be weeded from a particular subject area, and it might make the participants more willing to take part in this project. However, there's rarely a total match between the size of the various subject areas of the collection and the various levels of subject expertise on the staff. It's usually possible to give each person at least some subject areas in which they feel proficient, but undoubtedly some will have to review areas that are less familiar. Assigning some people areas outside their expertise can be more palatable if the person planning and administering the project weeds some of these hard-to-assign areas and if the participants feel that assignments have been made in a fair manner.

Another way to divide up the assignments so that the work is fairly distributed is to assign people to weed for a set number of hours per day or week. Each person would begin where the previous weeder had stopped. If the time allotted for this project is too short to allow only one person to weed at any given time, this can be overcome by beginning the weeding in more than one place within the reference collection. More important, this method would lose the advantages of having subject experts involved in the weeding project. Nevertheless, in some libraries this might be the most practical method of conducting a weeding project.

In addition to the people who will review the collection, there must also be a person who is responsible for the clerical part of the review or for supervising those who perform these tasks. Books that have been marked for weeding may need to be pulled from the shelves, put in an area where they can be reviewed, properly marked to ensure that each volume is sent to the correct destination, and moved to the appropriate location for the next step of processing.

Unless the library is very small, there will almost certainly be people from other departments who are expected to do some of the work involved in weeding a collection. After the final decision about which volumes will be weeded, somebody has to do technical processing and somebody needs to dispose of the weeded volumes, whether they are to be moved to some other location or withdrawn. Usually the person planning the project will discuss the proposed time line of the project with the relevant departments so they can plan for the disruption of their workload. In some cases, the reference weeding project may need to be rescheduled because one or more of the affected departments can't accommodate the additional work anticipated from the project during the time planned for the project.

The participants should have access to a list of the books that ought to be on the shelf. This used to be done from a card shelf list, but few libraries have such shelf lists these days. In many integrated library systems, a list can be created that includes all of the items that should be on the shelf, in call number order. If possible, this list should include title, date of publication, and usage data for each volume. It would be ideal if detailed usage data by year were available, but that may not be possible. By evaluating the list before going to the shelf to weed, the reviewer can mark those items that should be examined for removal from the reference collection. The list of books that ought to be on the shelf can be taken into the stacks as a card file or a printed list, or could be on a laptop, notebook, tablet, or other handheld device. An advantage to taking a computer into the stacks is that the reviewer has the ability to check entries in lists of recommended reference sources, such as the Guide to Reference (www.guidetoreference

.org), or to look up book reviews. The agreed-upon criteria to evaluate books should be available to the reviewers to carry into the stacks, either as a paper document or as a document on the computer or handheld device.

In addition to recommending that a book should be removed from the reference collection, the reviewer should also recommend a disposition for the book. Books could be sent to the circulating collection or another library collection, transferred to a storage facility, or withdrawn from the library collection entirely. An easy method for designating the proposed disposition of each book is to put a color-coded, labeled flag in the book that lists the recommended disposition of the book. The simplest method of removing the books from the shelves is for the person doing the review to remove them. However, if reviewers are reluctant to be part of the project, not being required to move books might eliminate one source of reluctance. Some reviewers might have back problems or other physical reasons that would make it difficult to repeatedly move heavy reference books or push full book carts. The books that have been flagged could be left on the shelf. Somebody else could come behind the reviewers and pull the flagged books, moving them to a place where they can be reviewed. Using the flags ensures that the correct books will be pulled from the shelf and that each book will have the appropriate color-coded flag giving the proposed disposition of the book.

If the reviewer is using a laptop, the list of books to be reviewed could be presented as a spreadsheet or database, and the reviewer could mark the list with some designation for each volume that should be removed. This has the advantage that no visible flags are left in the stacks. If the library is concerned that some library users would question the appropriateness of a weeding project, this method might be preferable. Color-coded flags could be added to the books once they have been removed from the stacks, if this is desired. The books could instead be divided onto shelves or carts that have each been designated for a particular kind of disposition.

A common practice is to allow the entire reference staff the opportunity to review books that have been recommended for removal from the collection. This is also an opportunity to have books reviewed by other members of the library staff—or by people outside the library, when appropriate. Shelves or book carts can be designated as review areas. It's helpful to put up a sign saying how long the books will be available for review. If only the reference staff will be reviewing the books, one week of review time is usually adequate, except at very busy times of the year or at a time when many people will be on vacation. If others will be reviewing them, a longer period may need to be assigned. It's important to inform the reviewers when these books are ready for evaluation. There should be flags or forms available that can be used by reviewers to recommend a different disposition for a volume other than that recommended by the initial reviewer. Some individual—probably the librarian responsible for the reference collection—should be designated to arbitrate any disputes and make the final decision. In some cases, a dispute may be resolved by referring to the reference collection development policy or to the policies and procedures being used for the review.

Some libraries prefer, or find it politic, to involve people outside the reference department or the library in the review. A school or college might wish to ask teachers or professors to review at least some items recommended for removal. A special library might wish to have other employees involved in the decision-making process. A public library might wish to have some community groups involved in specific parts of their review process. For instance, a public library might want to have a local genealogy group review the books that have been pulled from the genealogy/local history reference collection. Inviting people outside the library to be involved is very much a double-edged sword. Having the benefit of others' subject expertise can be valuable, but some people don't believe any books should be withdrawn from a library collection. Involving users in weeding projects carries the risk that the library will be the recipient of some critical, unwanted public scrutiny. However, in some cases, there may be people outside the library who are allowed, or even required, to review any books that have been designated to be withdrawn. For instance, in some school systems, the principal or an employee at the school administration office may have the responsibility of performing this evaluation.

Once all reviewers have had an opportunity to review the collection, the books are ready to be taken to the next venue for further processing. What steps must be taken and who is responsible for performing them will vary from library to library. Many technical services departments will want each book to be accompanied by a transfer or withdrawal form. However, some libraries may have shelves designated for books that are to be transferred or withdrawn, and the books can be placed on these shelves or carts without needing special forms. Alternatively, the project manager may be able to negotiate with technical services for books to be processed without individual transfer or withdrawal forms if they are delivered on book carts, with each cart holding only books that are to be transferred to a single location or withdrawn.

The library may have a general policy concerning the disposition of books that are withdrawn. If not, the plan for the weeding project should include what the library will do with the reference books that are withdrawn. Some libraries put these books out for the book sale or sell them to a company. They may be donated to another library, placed on book carts with a sign indicating they are free to anybody who wants them, or donated to a charitable organization. In some cases, books are sent to recycling facilities or put in a dumpster. One consideration in deciding how to dispose of withdrawn books is that books that are disposed of in any way that members of the public can acquire them, even if the library's ownership marks have been covered up and the books have been stamped *discarded* or *withdrawn*, may be returned to the library by helpful people who think they've found a book that was stolen.

Weeding library books can sometimes create a public relations problem. Putting books in a dumpster or recycling bin is more likely to be controversial than moving them to a storage facility. Few libraries want to see an article in the local press that says the library has discarded "thousands and thousands" of books, or that it "took them off the shelves and dumped them," or that compares the library's weeding program to Ray Bradbury's novel *Fahrenheit 451*.[9] Having seen press reports of people picketing libraries to protest weeding, checking the library dumpster to see if books have been discarded, or complaining to the press about weeding, it's no wonder some librarians prefer to keep tangible evidence of a weeding project as invisible as possible.

As one of the end products of a review, there should be procedures for reviewers to recommend books or other resources to be purchased. Some of the goals of a review might be to discover missing volumes, identify newer editions, or identify subject areas that need to be expanded. If these are goals for this project, it will not be finished until these tasks have been completed.

Some librarians enjoy weeding, but for many it is considered to be a tedious, unpleasant task. Planning the project should include trying to make the process as easy and pleasant as possible for everybody involved. In addition to maintaining open lines of communication so everybody involved is kept informed about the project, it never hurts to bring food to the meetings for a weeding project. The participants can celebrate how much progress has been made, congratulate one another on how hard they've worked, or condole with those who still have substantial weeding to be completed. In order to demonstrate how much progress has been made, some type of tangible representation might be placed in a staff area or a digital representation might be made available. In the staff area, this could be represented by a poster with a thermometer on it, similar to those used for fund-raising campaigns. An alternative would be to display posters or bulletin boards that contain a list of the sections to be reviewed. The reviewer could cross out each section when it is completed. Instead of a list, each section could be represented by a paper strip. As each section is finished, the reviewer could tear off the piece of paper for that section and throw it away. Depending on how happy the reviewer is to finish that section, she could tear up the paper or even put it through a shredder. A digital representation could provide the same information, but might not provide the same satisfaction as shredding a representation of the section that's been completed.

When the project is done, the reference department could have a party to celebrate finishing such an onerous task. Even if there's no celebration, the person in charge of the weeding project should acknowledge the hard work that each person did to contribute to the successful completion of this project.

Performing a Continuous Review of the Collection

Instead of weeding a large reference collection as a major project, some reference collection managers prefer to perform a continuous review of the reference collection. A 2009 survey of academic and public libraries in New York revealed that 41.3 percent of respondents, including 46.5 percent of public libraries and 32.6 percent of academic libraries, reported conducting a continuous review of the reference collection.[10]

The basic steps that need to be taken to perform the review are still primarily the same as those for weeding the collection as a major project. The ground rules must be set for the project. The project will need to be planned. The weeding will have to be completed and there will still be some cleanup before the project is completed. However, fewer people usually need to devote a substantial amount of their time to this type of review. The initial review could be performed by the librarian in charge of the reference collection, or this duty might be divided among all reference staff or among volunteers. Each reviewer could perform the initial review for one or more segments of the collection. Much of the plan for doing a review as a major project can be used for a continuous review. The reviewer can use the same criteria and the same forms or flags in individual books, and can either leave the books on the shelf for somebody else to pull or remove the books and place them on designated shelves. The reference staff can still have time to review the books that have been recommended for removal from the collection. The main difference in this method is that it is done a section at a time. The amount of time spent consulting with other departments of the library and coordinating with them is also much less. Because there aren't such tight time constraints, each batch of books removed from the collection may be much smaller, possibly only three to four shelves. These few books take little time for most reference librarians to review and take little extra time for other departments to process, so their workflow is less likely to be disrupted. After a short time, this type of review becomes part of the normal routine for everybody concerned. The main disadvantage is that this type of review can take a very long time to complete one pass through a large collection.

An alternative way to perform a continuous review is to designate a series of meetings to perform the review. This could be done as a part of each reference meeting. Somebody, probably the librarian in charge of the reference collection, could be given the task of pulling several shelves of books for each meeting. Each title could be considered and, if necessary, somebody could be designated to check the availability of a newer edition or replacement title. This intensive review allows each reference librarian to see each title, increasing each librarian's knowledge of the contents of the reference collection. It requires a considerable investment of time by the reference staff and is probably most appropriate for those libraries who consider their print reference collection to be of primary importance in answering reference questions and where there is also sufficient staff time to be devoted to such a practice.

Which Method of Weeding the Collection Is Best?

There is no one method of weeding that is best for all libraries and all situations. The first choice to make is whether the weeding will be done as a major project or a continuous weeding program. In many libraries, the main consideration will be the time frame in which the weeding must take place.

Advantages of weeding as a major project include:

- The project is completed in a relatively short time.
- The project has a definite ending point.
- If the entire reference staff is involved, they will all learn more about the content of the collection.
- Because of the shorter time frame, the project may be completed during a time when the reference staff is usually less busy.
- Because of the shorter time frame, the project may be completed during a time when fewer users are in the library.

Disadvantages of weeding as a major project include:

- It disrupts the workflow of the reviewers.
- It disrupts the workflow of other departments in the library.
- Because time is short, it's more likely that books will be weeded that should be kept in the collection.
- Because time is short, there's little time to be thoughtful about decisions.
- Because time is short, it's less likely that others will be consulted about individual titles.
- Because time is short, reviewers are less likely to check for the availability of newer editions.
- Books to be reviewed can become a space problem in all the affected departments.
- The activity involved in a major weeding project is more likely to draw public attention.
- Withdrawing many books at one time may make administrators wonder how well the reference department has spent its budget.

Advantages of a continuous weeding project include:

- It can be made a part of the regular workflow, minimizing disruption to the reviewer(s).
- It can become part of the regular workflow for other departments in the library, minimizing the disruption of their workflow.
- Practice makes perfect: If one reviewer does most of the preliminary weeding, she can become a more experienced, faster weeder.
- Because the project never ends, it ensures that all parts of the reference collection will be weeded on a somewhat regular basis.
- Because there's more time, the reviewer should have time to consult outside experts.
- Because there's more time, the reviewer should have time to be more thoughtful.

Disadvantages of a continuous weeding project include:

- It never ends.
- If the collection is large, it can take a very long time to weed the entire reference collection.
- Because it takes so long to weed an entire collection, there are always areas of the collection that are in serious need of immediate weeding, even though it may not be their turn for months.
- Because it takes so long to weed an entire collection, there may never be a time when the reference collection manager feels the entire print reference collection is in good shape.
- If only one person does the preliminary weeding, the reference staff may not be engaged in the project and may learn little about the content of the collection.

Reviewing Print Reference Serials

During the process of weeding items that are already on the reference shelves, some issues of reference serials may be removed from the collection. In addition to weeding the issues that have been received, the titles that are currently received as reference serials should also be reviewed periodically. If some titles are no longer needed, a decision can be made to cancel them before they are received, which could be considered pre-weeding, as it eliminates unneeded volumes before they must be weeded.

As part of the preparation for a review of serial items, a list of the titles received for the reference collection should be compiled. It's important that everybody involved in the decision-making process has accurate information about what titles are being evaluated. The list should include the title, call number, and several years of cost and usage data.

Usage data of serial titles may be problematic, depending on how the library collects this data. Earlier in this chapter, various methods of keeping usage statistics for the reference collection were listed. Usage statistics for serials may be kept in the integrated library system, as they are for reference monographs. In some libraries, usage data for serials may be more difficult to access than those for monographs. If a serials title is replaced each year by a new edition, usage data may cover only the most recent volume. If the newest volume was received only a few months ago, the usage data may be inadequate for making a decision about whether the title should be continued. Some serials are received in monthly issues, which are replaced by quarterly or annual volumes. As the monthly issues are discarded, the usage data for these issues may also be discarded, leaving the reviewer with incomplete data.

As in any review, one of the goals is to make this process as easy and painless as possible for those involved. Reference serials generally represent titles that the reference staff is accustomed to using and may have used for many years. Particularly if cuts will be necessary, some people can be very protective of their favorite reference serials, even when they haven't used a particular title in years. If some members of the group that will be reviewing serials are reluctant to cancel titles, an easy first step in the process is to have each participant review the list of reference serials and mark those they have used in the most recent year or two. These items can be removed from the list, at least for the moment, and the new list can be sent to members of the reference staff for evaluation. In the second round, participants can be asked to indicate items that could be canceled. This data can be added to the list of titles that are still under consideration. Beside each title, the number of people who indicated the title should be canceled can be given, and the new list can be sent to the participants. The discussion about what should be canceled could begin by considering the titles that were marked for cancellation by the greatest number of people, then those marked for cancellation by the second greatest number, and so forth.

In an ideal world, the budget would allow new resources to be added, but a more common goal is to make cuts in the reference serials budget. Even when there is an adequate budget to continue receiving all reference serials, the titles received should be reviewed periodically. It's much too easy to continue receiving titles that are no longer needed simply because they arrive automatically. A regular review can help keep serials from becoming a future weeding problem.

Weeding Reference Books in Off-Site Storage

Theoretically, weeding print reference materials that are housed in off-site storage facilities should be similar to reviewing the print reference collection in the library. This might be the case if the off-site storage facility is conveniently located and the facility's shelving is arranged so reviewers can access the facility and browse the shelves. However, many off-site storage facilities have compact shelving that may be as much as thirty-five feet high. Those allowed to retrieve materials from this type of shelving may have to be buckled into a special harness as a safety measure. In this type of facility, it won't be possible for librarians to physically review the books on the shelves. In addition, many storage facilities don't shelve reference materials in a separate part, but intermingle them in with other materials sent there for storage.

The first obstacle that must be overcome in reviewing reference materials that are housed in an off-site storage facility may be making a list of the titles that should be reviewed. Integrated library systems generally have location codes that designate where each item is housed. There will be codes for the reference collection, the indexes, and other reference locations. However, when an item is transferred to an off-site storage facility, it may be given a new location code that indicates only that it is housed there. Depending on the capabilities of the system and the decisions made about the availability and designation of location codes, there may not be a location code for reference materials at the storage facility. In some libraries the record for the item might include a code that indicates where the item was housed before being transferred to the storage facility. If the book had been first transferred to the circulating collection, there may be no indication in the item record to indicate the book was previously housed in the reference collection. If there is no code to indicate that an item currently housed in off-site storage was previously part of the reference collection, it may not be possible to produce an accurate, complete list of reference materials that are housed at a storage facility.

If it's not possible to produce a list of books that used to be part of the reference collection but are currently shelved in a storage facility from the ILS, the reference collection manager will have to investigate other methods of making such a list. One method might be to list records for titles that list some volumes in the reference collection and some volumes at the storage facility. Another method would be to produce lists of titles of types of reference books, such as encyclopedias, dictionaries, handbooks, and directories. Because some of these titles were probably never part of the reference collection, before the list is used for weeding, it should be reviewed to remove titles that were unlikely to have been part of the reference collection.

The review of this part of your reference collection may have to be accomplished by creating the most accurate and complete list possible and then using as many of the criteria for weeding as is practical. One factor that should be easy to determine is the amount of use received by each item since it was sent to the storage facility, because most storage facilities keep meticulous records of which items circulate. It might be possible for some items to be retrieved from the shelves for the weeding project, but this can be a cumbersome task in many storage facilities, so items should be requested only when necessary. Given only the information in the record for the item, these criteria should be easy to determine:

- Lack of use
- Lack of presence on standard lists of recommended sources
- Age of materials
- Availability of newer edition(s)
- Number of copies available
- Language of book

The following items will be more difficult to determine:

- Comprehensiveness of information
- Duplication of information in other sources
- Lack of citation to reference sources
- Condition of the book
- Usefulness for circulating collection

This review may be done by the librarian responsible for the reference collection, or the list could be divided and some of the initial review could be done by subject specialists. Once the initial review is completed, other members of the reference staff could review the recommendations, if desired. As these books have previously been sent to off-site storage, any item being weeded will probably be withdrawn. Once the review is complete, the list of items to be withdrawn can be sent to the off-site storage facility, or items in the library's integrated library system could be marked for withdrawal.

Reviewing the Electronic Reference Book Collection

In addition to reviewing the print reference collection, it is equally important to review the electronic reference book collection. In a 2009 ARL survey, only 4 percent of respondents said their libraries have a policy on weeding electronic books.[11]

Many electronic reference books are acquired by the library in ways that prevent the reference collection manager or other members of the library staff from weeding these books. Staff members will probably not be able to weed individual books that are part of a subscription database, whether the subscription was acquired through a consortium or directly by the library. If the library purchased aggregated databases, staff members might have the ability to weed individual titles, either by suppressing the records for these titles or by removing the records from the database. If individual electronic reference books were purchased individually and are discoverable through a list of electronic resources and/or the integrated library system, library staff should be able to suppress the ILS records for the titles, remove them from the list of electronic resources, or both.

Many of the criteria used for weeding electronic books will be those used for the print collection, such as age, completeness, or inclusion in standard reviewing sources. Other criteria are unique to electronic formats, such as methods of discovery and access, adequacy of the user interface, and other criteria used in selecting electronic resources.

The amount of planning needed will depend on the size and complexity of the electronic reference book collection. If the collection is very small or if the portion of the collection that can be controlled by the library staff is very small, there may be little planning or implementation time necessary. If there are many electronic reference books whose access can be controlled, this project may require the involvement of many people, and the amount of time spent planning will be commensurately longer.

Obviously a reviewer can't look at physical books to perform a title-by-title review, so a list of the books to be reviewed must be produced. There's no need to include books in the list that are in databases in which the content is controlled by a database producer, vendor, or consortium. If the library has a list that includes all the available electronic reference books, this may be used as a basis for a list. Then, the titles that don't need to be reviewed could be removed from the list. Because electronic reference books were probably acquired in a variety of ways, it may be more practical to make a series of lists, or to use a combination of lists that include titles that were purchased individually and titles from each of the databases in which the content can be controlled by the library.

At a minimum, these lists should include the catalog record number if available, the title, publisher, date of publication, usage data if available, and database in which the title is included, if relevant. There should be places for the reviewers to indicate which volumes should be weeded and which should be replaced with a more current volume.

Once the answers to the review have been compiled, the compiled lists can be made available to all reference and/or collection development librarians for review. After a final decision has been made, the method of deleting the book or the records for the book will vary depending on the access and discovery methods used by the library and/or the database vendor. If the books are listed in the integrated library system, these records can be deleted or suppressed. If the books are included in a list of the electronic reference books available from the library, they can be removed from the list. If the title is part of an aggregated database in which each title must be individually purchased by the library, the database vendor may be able to delete the title from the list of those available to the library. If the library pays an annual maintenance fee that is based on the number of electronic books purchased by the library, removing individual titles that are no longer appropriate for the library's collection may result in a lower maintenance fee. A result of this review might be to purchase or obtain access to more recent editions of some of the titles that were withdrawn from the electronic reference collection.

Reviewing Reference Databases

Becky Albitz writes, "Because electronic resources are easy to use, available 24 hours a day, seven days a week, and accessible from on and off campus, they become part of the research culture of an institution. Students, faculty and librarians become acclimatized to certain products and services, and have no desire to lose access to any of them." She recommends holding an annual meeting to review databases.[12] If there isn't an annual database review meeting, some alternative schedule should be established.

Frequently, database vendors must be informed at least thirty days, if not ninety days, before the bill is due if the library wishes to cancel a database, depending on the terms of the license. Even if the library chooses not to hold a formal database review meeting, it is a good practice to review the list of available databases every year. Several things should be accomplished in this review. Each database should be examined to determine if it is still plays an important role in the library's suite of resources. The library's needs may have changed, the content or user interface of the database may have become more or less appropriate for the collection, or there may be a database that would be an improvement over a resource to which the library currently subscribes. When possible, all databases in a subject area should be reviewed together to look for unnecessary duplication or insufficient coverage. The total amount budgeted for databases may need to be reduced. Because databases normally increase in cost, some databases may need to be canceled even if the budget for databases remains constant. Hoffmann and Wood write, "Due to cost, or cost per use, of virtual database licenses vis-à-vis library funds, deselection is a real consideration for licenses charged in whole or in part to the school library budget. The cost of full-text article databases is particularly vulnerable to increases because their content normally grows as the weekly, monthly, quarterly, or special issues of the journal titles are added to the database." They listed other reasons to cancel databases to include cost per use, content overlap between two databases, reduction in quality and content of a database, and replacement of a local database by a statewide database.[13]

A list of the databases to which the library subscribes should be produced before the database review meeting. The reference collection manager may not have to compile the data that is needed for a database review. This may be the responsibility of collection development, acquisitions, serials, or electronic resources librarians. At a minimum, this list should include the title of the database, the database producer, the annual cost, and any usage data. Other information that may be useful includes whether the price listed is for a subscription or annual maintenance fee (for titles that were purchased), database vendor, number of simultaneous users allowed, and subject area. Most of this information should be easy to find, but finding usage data for making decisions can be difficult. If possible, the most recent several years of usage data and database cost should be included because this will show trends. The cost per use for each of these time periods can also be very helpful for spotting trends in the continuing usefulness of a database. If the cost-per-use ratio goes up for several years, the database may be a candidate to consider for cancellation, or at least to put on a watch list. If similar databases will be compared, a comparison of the content will also be useful.

Finding comparable usage data can be difficult. Different database vendors provide usage data in different formats or have different definitions for terms, so each must be investigated individually in order to pull out the available usage data. Although usage data is valuable, it must be analyzed with other information. A database might have high usage because it's very useful or because users find it difficult to use and have to perform multiple searches to find useful information.

Once the data has been found, it must be analyzed to determine what it means and how it compares to the data from the other database producers. More database producers now follow the COUNTER standards, but comparing usage of several databases can still be a challenge. Nevertheless, whatever usage statistics are available for the databases to be reviewed must be gathered. Vendor-supplied usage data may be e-mailed to a designated person in the library or may be available on a password-protected Internet site. Compiling this data into a usable form for those who will be responsible for reviewing databases can be very time consuming.

If the selectors will have the opportunity to choose new databases, information should be gathered on the titles to be considered for purchase. Ideally, there will already have been a trial of each database under consideration.

If a group is going to perform this review, all the relevant information should be sent to them at least one week before the meeting so they can be prepared to have an informed discussion. Everybody who will be involved should be informed of how much money will be available, whether databases must be canceled, and whether the library will be able to add databases to the collection.

The meeting can include a review of the individual titles and of the entire group of databases. This may also be an appropriate meeting at which to discuss changes in the parent organization that will necessitate some adjustments to the suite of databases. The mission of a government agency or organization may have changed. The company may be shifting its business into new areas. A school or college curriculum may have been altered. The population profile of a public library's district may have been changed. There are many kinds of changes in a library's user population that might influence the exact mix of databases that ought to be provided. A reference collection is a living entity and must be reviewed on a regular basis in order to remain relevant to the user population.

A 2010 ARL library survey asked participants to list what activities were parts of the process for assessing whether to renew electronic resources. The activities most commonly part of the review process were:

- Assessing cost increases in the most recent year (48 percent)
- Assessing the history of cost increases (25 percent)
- Assessing the history of usage statistics (25 percent)
- Looking for availability from other sources (18 percent)
- Checking the availability of content in other library-owned electronic resources (16 percent)
- Determining the cost per use (16 percent)[14]

The participants were also asked to list what criteria in the process were most important. The most common deal breakers were cost (39 percent) and "compatibility with library systems" (12 percent). Many more criteria were rated as very important. The most common of these were:

- Relevance to current curricula (49 percent)
- Relevance to current faculty research (47 percent)
- Uniqueness of content (46 percent)
- Inflation history (43 percent)
- Cost per use (42 percent)[15]

Still Reluctant to Weed?

There are many reasons for being reluctant to weed the reference collection. A librarian who has trouble weeding is certainly not alone. The library literature is full of articles that say many librarians find it difficult to weed their collections.

Diane Young describes an eight-step system for those who find it difficult to weed:

1. Admit that you are emotionally attached to your collection.

2. Recognize that space is finite and overabundance can be a detractor.

3. Seek the help of experts to overcome your reluctance to judge.

4. Acknowledge to yourself and your colleagues that you've made selection mistakes.

5. Find ways to ease the anxiety of decision making.

6. Take the drudgery out of weeding.

7. Protect yourself from criticism through policies and PR.

8. Channel your love of books into finding good homes for your discards.[16]

In an attempt to encourage librarians in Florida's school library systems to weed, SUNLINK created the popular Weed of the Month program. Each month from September 1997 to December 2005, the program's website included directions for weeding a particular subject. Donna Baumbach and Linda Miller published *Less Is More,* a book based on this program.

Another method of easing into the practice of weeding is to start by doing onion weeding. This method is intended to increase a reviewer's comfort level with removing books from the collection. Take a section of the collection and peel off one layer at a time. Start by removing books that seem to be easy choices. What's considered an easy choice will vary from one librarian to another. It might be books that are more than five years old and also have never been *reshelved*, previous editions of reference books, books that are also available online, family medical guides more than five years old, or any book with a visible pile of dust on top. Once that layer of books has been removed, decide on another type of book that seems to be an easy category and peel off another layer, and then another layer. Most librarians, as they gain experience in weeding, find that practice may not make perfect, but it does result in a greater level of comfort with making decisions about what to remove from the reference collection. Experience generally helps a librarian make weeding decisions more quickly and with less agonizing over whether the right decision has been made.

NOTES

1. Maria Isabel Fernandes, "Ready Reference Collection: Thoughts on Trends," *Community & Junior College Libraries* 14 (2008): 205.
2. Jane T. Bradford, "What's Coming Off the Shelves? A Reference Use Study Analyzing Print Reference Sources Used in a University Library," *Journal of Academic Librarianship* 31 (November 2005): 550–551.
3. Nicole Heintzelman, Courtney Moore, and Joyce Ward, "Are Reference Books Becoming an Endangered Species? Results of a Yearlong Study of Reference Book Usage at the Winter Park Public Library," *Public Libraries* 47 (September/October 2008): 62–63.
4. Jeannie Colson, "Determining Use of an Academic Library Reference Collection: Report of a Study," *Reference & User Services Quarterly* 47 (Winter 2007): 170.
5. Donna J. Baumbach and Linda L. Miller, *Less Is More: A Practical Guide to Weeding School Library Collections* (Chicago: American Library Association, 2006), 4.
6. Polly Frank, Lee-Allison Levene, and Kathy Piehl, "Reference Collegiality: One Library's Experience," *Reference Librarian* 15 (1991): 40–41.
7. Juleigh Muirhead Clark and Karen Cary, "An Approach to the Evaluation of Ready Reference Collections," *Reference Services Review* 23 (Spring 1995): 39–43.
8. Paul H. Mosher, "Managing Library Collections: The Process of Review and Pruning," in *Collection Development in Libraries: A Treatise*, ed. Robert D. Stueart and George B. Miller Jr. (Greenwich, CT: JAI Press, 1980), 159–181.
9. Mark Sommer, "Book Weeding, Changes Stir Debate at Central Library," *Buffalo News*, Jan. 21, 2011, www.buffalonews.com/city/communities/buffalo/article319047.ece; Lisa Rein, "Hello, Grisham—So Long, Hemingway?" *Washington Post*, Jan. 2, 2007, www.washingtonpost.com/wp-dyn/content/article/2007/01/01/AR2007010100729.html; Tiffany Mayer, "Vetting of Books at School Library Peeves Volunteer," *The Standard* (St. Catherines, Ontario), April 4, 2009, www.thepeteroroughexaminer.com/ArticleDisplay.aspx?archive=true&e=1510901.
10. Jane Kessler, "Print Reference Collections in New York State: Report of a Survey," *Journal of the Library Administration and Management Section* 6 (March 2010): 37.
11. Catherine Anson and Ruth R. Connell, *E-book Collections*, SPEC Kit 313 (Washington, DC: Association of Research Libraries, 2009), 32.
12. Becky Albitz, *Licensing and Managing Electronic Resources* (Oxford, England: Chandos Publishing, 2008), 136.
13. Frank W. Hoffmann and Richard J. Wood, *Library Collection Development Policies: School Libraries and Learning Resource Centers*, Good Policy, Good Practice Series, No. 2 (Lanham, MD: Scarecrow Press, 2007). 153.
14. Richard Bleiler and Jill Livingston, *Evaluating E-resources*, SPEC Kit 316 (Washington, DC: Association of Research Libraries, 2010), 58–59.
15. Ibid.
16. Diane J. Young, "Get to Effective Weeding," *Library Journal*, Nov. 15, 2009, 36.

FOR FURTHER INFORMATION

Dubicki, Eleonora. "Weeding: Facing the Fears." *Collection Building* 27 (2008): 132–135.

Larson, Jeannette. *CREW: A Weeding Manual for Modern Libraries* 2008. www .tsl.state.tx.us/ld/pubs/crew/.

McCormack, Nancy. "When Weeding Hits the Headlines: How to Stop Your Library from Making (That Kind of) News." *Feliciter*, November 2008, 277–278.

Singer, Carol A. "Weeding Gone Wild: Planning and Implementing a Review of the Reference Collection." *Reference & User Services Quarterly* 47 (2008): 256–264.

Slote, Stanley J. *Weeding Library Collections: Library Weeding Methods.* Englewood, CO: Libraries Unlimited, Inc., 1997.

8

Reference Collection Development and Consortia

MEMBERSHIP IN LIBRARY consortia is an important component in the life of many libraries. In a 2010 survey of ARL libraries, all seventy-three respondents belonged to at least one consortium. Respondents were asked if they belonged to one or more consortia "for the primary purpose of acquiring commercially available e-resources." Seventy libraries answering yes to this question belonged to a mean number of 3.18 consortia.[1] Library consortia offer services and perform functions that have little to do with the reference collection, although these services and functions may be crucial to the success of reference services in the library. This chapter is concerned with the effect of membership in library consortia on reference collection development and management.

When reference collections were composed primarily of print resources, being a member of a consortium rarely had a significant effect on the development of a library's reference collection, because most libraries don't allow reference books to circulate. However, as reference collections have become more dominated by electronic resources, this situation has changed. Now, working with a consortium can be an important factor in developing and managing a reference collection.

Library consortia vary widely in purpose and influence, so some will have a more far-reaching effect than others. Some consortia serve only as a buying club. That is, they negotiate prices with database vendors, take care of licensing, and manage financial matters, but offer no other services.

Other consortia may offer a variety of services. Some of the more common services and functions offered by library consortia are to:

- Provide a consortium-wide OPAC
- Allow members of consortium member institutions to make direct requests online for books or other physical materials
- Deliver library materials among consortium libraries
- Allow users of consortium members to check out materials from any consortium library
- Run off-site storage facilities
- Coordinate collection development among consortium libraries
- Run a consortium-wide online reference service
- Negotiate licensing and prices for online resources
- Provide MARC records for member library catalogs for resources purchased and/or resources aggregated in a database that was purchased
- Provide for perpetual access to consortial e-resources
- Design and/or run federated search engines, discovery layers, databases, etc.
- Provide a portal to all consortium online resources
- Run a digital resource commons for materials from consortium libraries
- Coordinate or provide training to staff and/or users at consortium libraries

There are various ways in which consortia may fund online resources. The consortium may have a budget that includes funds supplied by consortium members, and sometimes by a state or local government. The consortium uses this money to acquire online resources that will be available to all consortium members. The consortium may also negotiate prices for online resources but not supply any of the money. Instead, consortium members who wish to take advantage of these lower prices will subscribe through the consortium. In this case, the final price for each library might depend on the number of libraries that subscribe. Some consortia also offer a funding model in which the consortium negotiates a price that would allow all members of the consortium to have access to the online resource, but the consortium does not supply any money. Instead, individual member libraries decide how much money they wish to contribute to the total cost of the resource. When, or if, the total amount of money needed to acquire the database is reached, all consortium libraries gain access to it, whether or not they contributed any money. In this scenario, if enough money was not provided by the member libraries, the deal would not be completed and the online resource would not be available through the consortium.

Budgeting for Reference Materials

When a library belongs to a consortium that purchases online reference resources for the entire membership of the consortium, the library usually has to pay a share of the cost of those resources. This share may be based on the number of potential library users, the number of books checked out, the size of the materials budget, or a combination of various factors. A major advantage of purchasing online reference resources through a consortium is that the consortium is generally able to negotiate a lower price—sometimes a significantly lower price—than most libraries would be able to negotiate individually. The price is usually even more advantageous when several consortia band together to negotiate for online resources. Purchasing through a consortium usually means a library is able to offer a greater number and variety of online resources than it would otherwise be able to provide.

In some libraries the entire reference budget, or at least the budget for online resources, may be allocated to the consortium, and the library may not be able to purchase any additional online reference materials. Because the prices negotiated by library consortia are usually so much lower than those that can be negotiated by an individual library, the library should still find that it can provide a greater number of online resources than it would have been able to afford if it had to negotiate on its own. A library that still has additional funds for online resources after paying its share of the consortium budget will need to make decisions about what additional online resources should be acquired after evaluating the mix of resources provided through the consortium or consortia to which they belong. In most cases, there's a balancing act between allocating money to the consortium and keeping funds for local purchases. On the one hand, it's smart to take advantage of the lower prices that are available by acquiring resources through the consortium, but there's also a need to design a collection that will most closely meet the needs of those who use the library.

When economic conditions are difficult and the materials budget for a consortium becomes tighter, the consortium must either cancel some resources or find a way to increase the amount of money available. To increase the budget, the consortium can ask the individual libraries for more money, or if some of the budget comes from another source such as state or local government, it can seek additional funding from the governmental entity. If at all possible, members of a consortium will want to avoid canceling online resources provided through the consortium because of the extremely favorable terms that have been negotiated for those resources. If the consortium has to cancel such a contract, it may not be able to negotiate a comparable contract when the budget is eventually increased. Individual libraries may also have to subscribe to some of these canceled resources, but will almost certainly have to do so at a considerably higher price. If an individual member library allocates additional money to the consortium to help it through a budget crisis, the library might have less money to be allocated to the reference budget. Even if the library provides more money to the consortium, the total amount of additional money allocated to the consortium by all members may still be less than that needed by the consortium to maintain all online resources. In this case, decisions must still be made by the consortium members to cancel some electronic resources. Either because the library has sent additional money to the consortium or because of individual database decisions made by the consortium members, locally purchased electronic resources may need to be reevaluated to determine if some must be canceled.

In most libraries, there is a limited amount of money for the materials budgets. Because money is sent to the consortium, there may be less money for the local reference budgets. This doesn't necessarily mean that the library will be able to provide fewer reference resources. It may mean just the opposite because of the greater purchasing power of a consortium. However, it does mean that decisions made by members of the consortium may have a direct impact on the reference budget and on the development of the reference collection.

Selection of Materials

Belonging to a consortium may mean that the reference collection manager has less control over the contents of the reference collection. The electronic reference resources purchased by the consortium are controlled by the consortium, although this may mean they were selected by a committee composed of reference and/or collection development librarians from members of the consortium. Nevertheless, even if the reference collection manager is a member of that committee, there are still many voices to be heard about what should be acquired by the consortium. Typically, this means that the materials purchased by the consortium will sometimes be resources the reference collection manager would buy for the reference collection and will sometimes be things that wouldn't be considered for acquisition, although these peripheral resources may prove to be more useful than expected. However, the prices negotiated by the consortium are usually so much lower than those that could be negotiated for an individual library that the library is frequently still paying less than the total cost would have been for only the resources that the reference collection manager would have chosen to acquire. In most cases, it's still financially favorable to belong to the consortium. Of course, a consortium may offer many additional services and benefits to members than simply the opportunity to purchase materials for a lower price.

In practical terms, having a suite of databases, electronic journals, e-books, and other resources that are made available through a consortium means that the selection of additional materials for the reference collection needs to be coordinated with the consortium resources. After the consortium has made its collection development decisions, the reference collection manager must analyze what reference resources are still needed to meet the needs of those who use the library. This might lead to purchasing materials for academic subjects taught at the institution or for topics demanded by the local community that aren't adequately covered by the resources acquired by the consortium. The library may need reference materials in languages other than those included in consortium resources. The library might serve a more diverse user community than that served by consortium members overall and require reference materials that reflect the needs of that community. Few consortia are composed of libraries that have identical plans for developing the reference collection, so it's unlikely the resources provided through the consortium will be a perfect match for any particular library reference collection.

Sometimes the consortium committee that chooses online resources must decide between two or more databases that are similar in scope and content. The librarians and library users at the library may have a definite preference for one of these databases. If the consortium committee chooses a different database, the reference collection manager and other library staff members may need to decide if the local preference is sufficiently pronounced that the library should acquire the preferred database, even though it will have access to a similar one through the consortium. Making these kinds of decisions requires considerable thought and discussion among all interested parties, because purchasing near-duplicate resources means the library won't be able to acquire some other resources. There's always an opportunity cost to any collection development decision, but the higher cost of most online resources means each decision carries with it a higher opportunity cost.

It's not uncommon for a consortium to subscribe to a suite of databases from one database vendor, as this can be a very cost-efficient way of providing access to databases. This suite of databases usually provides a core of heavily used databases but also contains some more specialized databases. The consortium may also provide access to more specialized resources to complement this foundation. Individual member libraries can then acquire additional online resources to address local needs that were not sufficiently addressed by the online resources available from the consortium.

Sometimes the consortium decides to replace the current suite of databases with a suite from another database vendor. Usually, the new suite of databases will include a similar group of core, heavily used databases, but the specialized databases will probably not include the same mix of subjects that were included in the previous suite of databases. This can result in a domino effect of database changes when the library's collection development staff, including the reference collection manager, must make changes in local database subscriptions as a result of the changes at the consortium level.

An occasional complication to negotiating individually for a database is that the consortium begins negotiations for the same database. If a library within the consortium acquires the database prior to or during the negotiations for the database, the consortium might not be able to negotiate as advantageous a price. If the library has already begun negotiations for an electronic resource and the consortium starts negotiations, it may be wise to delay the library's negotiations, both as one facet of being a good citizen of the consortium, and also in the hope that the consortium will be able to negotiate a more advantageous price.

There is sometimes a conflict between being a good citizen of a consortium and providing resources as quickly as possible. When there is a library staff member or a library user who is very eager to get access to a particular online resource, it can be difficult to convince that person that it will be better to wait for the final outcome of consortium negotiations. This situation can be exacerbated when consortium negotiations become protracted. The reference collection manager must weigh the importance of providing the library's users with an immediate addition to the collection against the potential benefits of waiting for the consortium to conclude the decision-making process.

Consortium-Produced Databases

One particularly valuable service performed by some consortia is the production of aggregated databases. These may be aggregations of electronic journals, books, dissertations, video files, audio files, images, or other resources. The construction of a database composed of electronic reference books from multiple publishers can alleviate the disadvantages of purchasing multiple databases of aggregated content from individual publishers. If the consortium produces its own custom-aggregated database of electronic reference books from many publishers into a single database, that database becomes more valuable as a single source for access to reference book content. Another advantage of the consortium performing this service is that the members of the consortium staff who are designing the aggregated database are likely to be responsive to the suggestions of consortium library staff members who wish to provide input to improve the user interface and search functions of the database. In many consortia, input by consortium members is an integral part of the planning process for a consortium-produced database.

Off-Site Storage

Some off-site storage facilities are shared by two or more members within a consortium. In some cases, members of the consortium have decided that some or all of the collections at the storage facility or facilities will be owned by the consortium instead of by the individual libraries. Which parts of the collection become the property of the consortium and which remain the property of the individual libraries would depend on the terms of the agreements signed by the members of the consortium. Depending on these terms, materials from the reference collection might be exempt from the joint ownership agreement. However, some or all of the materials that were formerly part of the reference collection might be included in the joint ownership agreement. If this is the case, the library might lose the right to bring reference books back to be reintegrated into the reference collection. This doesn't necessarily mean that these reference books couldn't be returned to the library to be housed temporarily in the library that purchased them or in another member library. For instance, a set could be brought back to be put on reserve for a class or to be used for a special project. However, this might be permitted only as a temporary arrangement. An important consideration is that this type of arrangement might be possible for former reference materials from all consortium members. Library users might be able to request loans of reference materials that used to be owned by other libraries that belong to the consortium. This broader availability of reference materials formerly accessible only to users of a particular library may benefit scholars and other users of all consortium members.

It's common for a library to send paper indexes to an off-site storage facility when they are replaced by a database. Frequently, members of the reference department want to reserve the ability to bring back the paper copy if the library loses access to the database. If these indexes become owned by the consortium, the library that originally purchased the indexes would no longer be the owner of the indexes and wouldn't be able to reintegrate the indexes into the library's reference collection. This may or may not be a major disadvantage, depending on whether library users would be willing to use these older print indexes, even if access to the online version ceased. Alternatives to providing older print resources would be for the reference staff to encourage researchers to make use of the existing online resources provided by the library or to investigate the possibility of subscribing to a comparable online resource.

Because space at many off-site storage facilities is at a premium, and because some titles may be sent to storage facilities by multiple libraries within a consortium, some shared off-site storage facilities are beginning to remove duplicates from the shared collection. Some librarians are concerned that, when a collection becomes the property of the consortium, decisions about retention of duplicate materials will be made by the consortium, rather than by the libraries that originally purchased the reference materials. If numerous copies of the same encyclopedia or index were deposited in the jointly owned off-site storage facilities, the consortium might decide to withdraw the excess copies. The possibility that reference books could be withdrawn by the consortium with no input from the library that originally purchased the books may require a change in the way collection managers think about reference collections.

Pros and Cons of Working with a Consortium

Being a member of a consortium has advantages and disadvantages. One major advantage is that consortia can usually negotiate prices that are considerably better than the library collection manager could negotiate for his own library. Ivy Anderson of the California Digital Library explains some of the advantages of consortial acquisition of online resources: "A consortial agreement expands access in at least two ways: by negotiating lower prices and re-distributing costs, it can make resources affordable for its smaller members; and by offering 'cross access' to content subscribed to by other member institutions, it can make available to each member far more content than would be possible in an individual agreement." In addition to negotiating better prices, consortia are sometimes able to negotiate more favorable licensing terms.[2]

That means the library can provide a greater variety of resources for library users. When the consortium can provide the core databases at a much better price, the library may be able to provide access to more of the specialized databases that users want. Jennifer Duncan credits two consortia for giving her library "access to a wealth of databases that we never could have afforded had we been going it alone" and providing "access to our primary aggregator, which would otherwise consume the lion's share of our electronic budget." She concludes, "Because our statewide consortium picks up many general databases, we are able to use our funds for the specialized products that really fit with the curricular and research needs of our institution."[3] Even if a library has incredibly skilled and knowledgeable reference librarians, their ability to help users may be limited by a lack of available resources. The provision of a broader range of online resources by the consortium can have a direct positive effect on the quality of the reference service offered to those who use the library.

Some consortia also offer services, hardware, or software that make it possible for users to complete their research easier, faster, and/or more effectively, which may also impact the way the reference materials can be used. For instance, a consortium may provide server space that the library can't provide, but that may be used for electronic resources purchased by the library or for items that are part of a shared resource made available to all members of the consortium. The consortium may provide a discovery layer that will allow users to identify more of the materials that the library provides, increasing the use of reference materials. It might provide a common user interface for a suite of databases so that users don't have to learn as many different interfaces. It might create a federated search engine for articles, books, or other materials, encouraging use of a wider variety of the library's online resources. The consortium might provide bibliographic management software, allowing researchers to more efficiently organize the resources they have used. All these services can enhance the use of the reference collection and influence how that collection is developed.

For some libraries, the consortium is of more than average importance. A school library that has only one librarian and a very small budget may be totally dependent on the consortium to provide online resources. The small public or college library might not have the technical staff to manage electronic resources or staff with the knowledge and ability to negotiate licenses. Any library with a tight budget might find that a consortium is the best option for maximizing its budget to provide a much wider variety of resources than the library otherwise would be able to offer to its users.

As with any situation that has so many positive attributes, there can also be disadvantages or complications to being a member of a consortium. Some reference collection managers may feel the primary disadvantage is a loss of independence. Each member of a consortium has individual priorities, so no one library has the power to choose which resources will be purchased or what services will be provided. There are many voices, each of which represents a library with its own particular needs and desires. Compromise and collaboration are necessary for any consortium to be successful. Ashmore and Grogg explain that the disadvantages of consortial membership can be alleviated by carefully choosing the consortium to join: "Ultimately, the key to a successful consortium is a set of libraries that share a common set of goals." They quote Kim Armstrong, the assistant director of the Center for Library Initiatives at the Committee on Institutional Cooperation: "Trust is also a big deal. If you are going to ask libraries to do things, sometimes give up autonomy and time, for the greater good, they have got to trust each other and [trust] that the organization will help fulfill their mission."[4]

Being a Good Citizen of a Consortium

What does it mean to be a good citizen of a consortium? One facet of being a good consortium citizen is that members of the library staff need to volunteer to participate in consortium committees and task forces to evaluate specific resources and services, recommend solutions for problems, draft white papers and other documents, and take part in the work of the consortium. A consortium that uses committees to promulgate policy and make decisions will succeed only if staff members at member libraries are willing to make the commitment to contribute to the work of the consortium.

Consortia also need adequate funds to do their work. If the members of the library staff value the advantages of being a member of the consortium, it may mean the library will voluntarily increase the amount of money allocated to the consortium when budgets are tight so the consortium doesn't have to cancel a database and lose the very advantageous price they have negotiated. In a difficult economy, it is sometimes necessary to choose between acquiring a specialized database locally and supporting the acquisition of key resources at the consortium level.

Supporting a library consortium may occasionally mean choosing to suspend or delay local negotiations for a database until the consortium has concluded its negotiations with that database vendor. Sometimes it means putting the good of the consortium before a more immediate goal of the library, trusting that the end result will be advantageous to all members of the consortium, including your own library.

NOTES

1. Richard Bleiler and Jill Livingston, *Evaluating E-resources*, SPEC Kit 316 (Washington, DC: Association of Research Libraries, 2010), 12.
2. Beth Ashmore and Jill E. Grogg, "The Art of the Deal," *Searcher*, March 2009, 40–47.
3. Frances C. Wilkinson and Linda K. Lewis, "Buy One, Get One e—or Has Print Finally Become Never, No More In Reference Collections?" *Against the Grain*, September 2004, 22.
4. Ashmore and Grogg, "The Art of the Deal."

9

Discovery and Access

LIBRARIANS HAVE LONG struggled to find ways to ensure that the expensive reference resources they acquire can be found and used by their users. This was true when reference collections were totally print, and it is equally true today. Marks and Janke write, "The concept of discoverability is perhaps the biggest challenge . . . The challenge for librarians and publishers is how to work together to steer the end users to the content in a library setting."[1]

Discovering Print Reference Sources

Most librarians are so accustomed to identifying and accessing paper reference resources they don't think about how much work was needed to make this possible. Before reference collections could be useful, librarians had to invent a comprehensive, workable scheme to organize the books in the library and invent various methods for indexing or otherwise identifying which of the available reference resources would be useful for a particular question. The first of these was solved by designing complex systems of classification. Reference books were removed from the rest of the collection and organized using one of these classification schemes. A person who wanted to identify which reference books might be most useful could then browse the shelves and expect to find similar books near each other. The second part of this process was to make these books discoverable by designing catalogs that listed the available books and permitted access by such attributes as author, title, and subject. Many of the early catalogs were in the form of books. In the quest to find improved methods of accessing their collection, libraries switched to using a card catalog and then to an online catalog. Along the way, complex systems of controlled vocabulary were designed to describe the books, and the number of searchable fields for each title increased, allowing users to identify books in more sophisticated ways.

It's obvious that catalogs weren't completely adequate because there were so many subject bibliographies produced in order to gather together resources and provide specialized indexes that would make the most useful sources more easily identifiable. These subject bibliographies used to be a major component of many reference collections. Increasingly, many libraries have removed some or all of the subject bibliographies from the reference collection and sent them either to the circulating collection or to a storage facility as they received increasingly less use in the reference collection.

A key component of the discovery system for print reference books is the ability to physically browse the print reference collection. Any experienced reference librarian has learned where to look on the shelf for a field guide to birds or an encyclopedia of African American history, if the collection contains those resources. Although users are sometimes confused by the thousands of reference books they see on the shelves, librarians see not just the books, but the organizational scheme that governs the placement of books. Reference librarians create mental maps that show the location of various resources in their print reference collection. They might know that the books on a particular subject are at the end of the H's or in the 636s, or that a particular title is shelved at the end of the third range. At least, reference librarians *used* to make these mental maps of the print reference collection. In many libraries, the print reference collection receives so little use that some reference librarian's mental maps are getting rather faded from disuse.

Discovering Electronic Reference Sources

What librarians really need now are mental maps of the virtual reference collection or some substitute for those mental maps. However, there isn't any universal classification scheme for virtual reference sources. Librarians don't see these resources lined up on shelves. Instead, librarians must devise other ways of making electronic reference resources equally as discoverable and accessible as the paper reference resources.

One of the problems with identifying the most useful electronic reference resources for a particular information need is that these resources come to libraries in various forms. In some cases, the library purchases individual titles. Electronic reference resources are also acquired in aggregated databases, which may include one subject or many. Reference resources can be found in databases that include a variety of materials, not all of which are traditionally thought of as reference sources. Even if the database is categorized as a reference item, the changeability of online sources prevents a librarian from knowing the content of the reference collection in the same way a librarian used to know the content of the print reference collection. When a library purchases a book, the content doesn't change over time unless somebody tears out pages or the book is updated by supplements. The content of electronic resources can change at any time. The content can be revised, text or images can be removed, or other content may suddenly appear. Individual titles within an aggregated database can be removed or added. In many cases, the librarian not only has no control over this but isn't even notified that there have been additions or deletions. Because the content and user interface of electronic sources are so easily changed and are rarely controlled by the reference librarian, it's difficult for any librarian to know exactly what will be found in a particular source.

Another complication of using online reference sources is the array of freely available Internet sites that comprise a storehouse of potentially useful information, so vast and unorganized that it can seem to be an impossible task to discover what sites ought to be added to any organized collection.

Identifying Individual Databases

One solution libraries have found to identify individual databases or items acquired as single titles is to produce a list of these resources, by title and/or subject. Some libraries include at least some freely available Internet sources on this list. Less frequently, there may be a searchable database of databases, allowing the descriptions of the databases to be searched. Because the success of such a searchable database of databases depends heavily on the accuracy and completeness of the database descriptions, this is more satisfactory for databases that consist of resources that all center on an easily identifiable subject. However, it's a much less satisfactory solution for identifying interdisciplinary databases that might be useful.

A common method of identifying online resources is the online research guide. Many of these include a variety of formats on a particular topic or type of resource. This is also sometimes used to gather together freely available Internet resources into a type of collection. For instance, one

food and nutrition guide to resources (http://libguides.bgsu.edu/content
.php?pid=17100) includes a series of subject-oriented pages that list Internet resources that might be useful to reference librarians or to individual
users. Other pages list online and print reference books, databases that
index articles, aggregated databases of full-text books, and other resources
that might be helpful to students studying food and nutrition.

Online research guides can also be used to gather together a variety
of formats of a particular type of material. The guide Newspapers: Finding Current and Historical Newspapers (http://libguides.bgsu.edu/news
papers/) includes lists of databases that were acquired by the library as
annual subscriptions or with perpetual access, individual newspapers and
aggregated databases of newspapers that are freely available on the Internet, and newspapers owned by the library in paper, microfilm, microfiche,
and microcard.

An advantage of producing this type of online guide is that it can be tai-
lored to the particular needs and collections of an individual library. The
guide can also include information about how to use a particular resource
in addition to information about the content. A guide may also be primarily about how to use a resource, such as Bowling Green State University's
guide to Summon (http://libguides.bgsu.edu/summon/).

Identifying Individual Titles within a Larger Database

When a database consists of a variety of individually titled resources, many
libraries would like to also be able to provide a list of those titles, or at least
of the individual titles in some databases. For instance, a common feature
on library websites is a list of all journals that are available in full text in
any of the library's databases, along with information about each title that
might include available years, the extent of full text, and so on. If a library
provides access to only a small list of full-text journals, it might produce an
in-house list of these journals made with word processing or spreadsheet
software. As the number of available full-text journals and magazines has
increased, it's more common for libraries to purchase an electronic resource
management (ERM) system for this type of information.

However, databases contain text files other than journal articles, in addition to nontext files, such as image, audio, and video files. Any librarian
who is managing an electronic reference collection must decide how many
of these files should be individually identifiable and how this should best
be accomplished.

This isn't a new problem. As libraries continue to add online resources
to their collections and as more databases include a variety of individual

titles, librarians have struggled to find ways to make the individual titles discoverable. In 2002, Linda Keiter and Margaret Landesman, from the University of Utah, noted their library had chosen to list aggregated reference databases both by the title of the package and also by the titles of the individual items, in addition to including them in research guides. Their database of databases could also be searched by subject. Even after all this effort, they concluded, "It seems to us important to note that none of this ensures that users will find reference sources."[2]

Downloadable MARC records are available for the individual titles contained in some databases, and these records can be added to the library catalog. This can be the case for individual books, musical scores, poems, plays, journal titles, and similar items. Sometimes these catalog records are provided by the database producer for free or at an additional cost. If cataloging records are available, the primary method of discovering electronic reference resources might be the library catalog. In many catalogs, there is a limiter for the reference collection, which retrieves materials in the print reference collection, and a limiter to Internet sources, which retrieves all online resources, not just those that might be considered to be reference resources. However, in most catalogs there isn't a way to limit search results to only electronic reference sources or to only electronic reference books. The University of Kansas found one solution by adding the genre heading *electronic reference works* to the catalog record of each electronic reference book. This allowed a keyword search of *electronic reference works* to retrieve the records for all electronic reference books.[3]

Identifying individual electronic reference titles remains a problem in many libraries. Some libraries have purchased an ERM system that is meant to be used to manage access to these monographic electronic resources, just as it has for serial electronic resources. As the number of aggregated databases acquired by a library increases, it becomes more and more difficult to find the items that are most useful to answer a reference query. Instead of requiring the user to search for an individual title in multiple databases, this can provide a shortcut and improve the chance that these titles will be used.

Another solution to the problem of identifying individual online reference books was designed by librarians at Quinnipiac University (http://learn.quinnipiac.edu/verso/versomain.html). They imagined a digital reference shelf that would mimic the physical reference collection. When a library user clicks on the end of a range, labeled with a major subject, the database displays a series of book spines. Clicking on the book spine with the desired title displays the cover of the book. Clicking on the cover of the book allows access to the content.[4]

A 2009 ARL survey asked participants how users find the electronic books owned by the library. This survey referred to all electronic books, not just electronic reference books. Respondents listed various methods:

- Links to electronic book collections on the library Internet page (85 percent)
- Books listed individually in the library catalog (83 percent)
- Library catalog permits search/limit for online books (69 percent)
- Search in WorldCat (59 percent)
- Links in databases (55 percent)
- Notations for electronic books are added to catalog records (54 percent)
- Search engines, such as Google (52 percent)
- Electronic books are linked from a library web page (30 percent)
- Electronic books are linked from the course management system (28 percent)[5]

For an online resource that is an aggregated collection of reference books, using the library catalog as the primary method of discovery of the individual monographs might be an acceptable way to find the individual books. However, it may not be as effective at discovering the individual entries in a reference resource such as an online subject encyclopedia. Some records include the table of contents and/or a summary of the subject of the book, and these can be helpful in identifying appropriate sources. Unfortunately, these fields are not available for all reference books. For the library catalog to be the solution to finding content in the library's collection of electronic reference books, this type of metadata must be provided for a much higher percentage of catalog records.

Rarely does a reference librarian expect to use the entire text of a subject encyclopedia to answer a reference question. Usually she is looking for an entry on the topic. For instance, a user might ask for information on Tecumseh, but a reference librarian will usually not expect to find an entire print or electronic subject encyclopedia on only a single person. Instead, the librarian might go to a biographical directory of famous Americans, an encyclopedia on wars in the United States, or a book about the history of Native Americans. John East describes some problems with the use of individual subject encyclopedias: "To be used, they must be online. But being online is not enough: they must be easily findable and ideally cross-searchable so that we can leverage the variety of content and viewpoint in our entire electronic encyclopedia collection . . . The alternative is to accept that the encyclopedia no longer has a place in today's information environment."[6]

Some libraries have resolved this problem by subscribing to Reference Universe (http://refuniv.odyssi.com), a database that searches for individual entries in the electronic and print books that are part of a library's reference collection. Other libraries, or library consortia, have tried to solve the problem by producing an aggregated database of electronic reference books, from various database providers. This can allow the full text, titles of entries, or other components of the books to be searched.

There is a school of thought that says anything in a database can be used as a reference source, even if it wasn't designed specifically as a reference source. This is a much broader definition of what is included in a library's reference collection than that used by the creators of Reference Universe or of an aggregated database of reference books. Librarians, who regard all online sources as potential reference sources, might answer questions by searching a wide variety of individual databases, many of which would not be categorized as reference databases. A librarian trying to identify a quotation might use full-text databases of books, poetry, articles, plays, speeches, or the Bible, or might do a search of the Internet, instead of using a quotation book. A chemist looking for a description of a particular chemical process might search a database of chemistry books, instead of going to a chemical handbook.

One recent option for libraries that wish to provide quick, easy access to both reference and nonreference resources might be to use a discovery layer to allow librarians and library users to identify relevant information in the library's tangible and virtual collections.

Web-scale Discovery

The use of web-scale discovery is increasingly popular in libraries, although these products are still quite new in the library world. The key idea behind these products is that they provide a single search interface that integrates searching for books, journals, and other resources found in a library catalog, but also includes searching resources from a wide variety of databases and other online providers. This database can provide access to a large portion of the resources made available by the library, providing what seems to be a one-stop shop for researchers.

One of the things that separate these products from federated search engines is that federated search engines search a variety of databases by sending a search query to each database and then compiling the answers. Instead, most web-scale discovery products work by first compiling a huge database of resources and then by indexing the database. When a researcher performs a search, he or she is searching the database that has been previously compiled by the web-scale discovery producer, instead of searching a series of databases. Because the database that is being used has already been compiled, the search is usually much faster than a federated search.

Because a web-scale discovery product searches such a large database, the user is likely to believe that all relevant library resources have been searched. However, this database will likely not include all resources made available by the library. Each web-scale discovery company signs contracts with many publishers in order to provide as large a database as possible, but the library will probably have access to resources from publishers with which the company has not signed a contract.

When considering the purchase of discovery software, part of the decision-making process is probably determining which of the library's electronic resources are included in each web-scale discovery database that is under consideration. Once a library has purchased web-scale discovery software, the collection development staff might want to include the presence of the potential acquisition, or the presence of the individual titles from the online resource, in the web-scale discovery database as one factor in choosing new electronic resources.

Many libraries make their web-scale discovery database the default search on the library home page. As this product becomes more heavily used, it will inevitably change the use patterns for electronic resources. Use of resources that are not part of the discovery database will likely decrease, which may necessitate some cancellations. Some databases for which the library has acquired only a limited number of seats may become more heavily used, causing a reconsideration of whether the library should pay to make the database available to additional simultaneous users.

One of the strengths of a web-scale discovery database is that it searches across a very large, multidisciplinary database. Due to the multidisciplinary nature of the product, a discipline-specific controlled vocabulary, such as a researcher would find in a database such as PubMed or PsycINFO, does not exist. Much of the content may be present in the database, but the search capabilities will be quite different.

These databases also don't offer the specialized search features of some subject databases. For instance, a researcher looking for case law won't find special search boxes devoted to this type of search. A search for information on the psychology of teenagers won't be able to include a limit for that specific age group. They don't offer the options of a business database to limit the search to SWOT analyses or company reports.

Because web-scale discovery is so new, there are still questions to be answered about how well this software will serve the needs of librarians and library users to find reference resources. Jason Vaughan writes, "The ultimate goal of any discovery service, bar none, is to place content in the hands of the user or, more specifically, to discover, present, and deliver relevant content in a convenient, intuitive manner to today's researcher."[7] Jeff Wisniewski describes web-scale discovery as "both a next-generation OPAC and federated search system (on steroids)."[8] Luther and Kelly caution, "The new unified-index discovery tools offer great potential for simplifying scholarly search and making it more effective. As with all technology solutions, however, myriad details need to be sorted out in the move from concept to operational success. And the differences in how these tools are being implemented have implications for both libraries and for the publishers that supply the information.[9]

NOTES

1. Jayne Marks and Rolf A. Janke, "The Future of Academic Publishing: A View From the Top," *Journal of Library Administration* 49 (2009): 456.
2. Frances C. Wilkinson and Linda Lewis, "Would You Like Print With That?— Will Electronic Reference Packages Supplant Print?" *Against the Grain*, September 2002, 18.
3. Sara Morris, Frances Devlin, Judith Emde, and Kathy Graves, *Reference E-Books: The Other Hidden Collection*, 2010, http://kuscholarworks.ku.edu/dspace/bitstream/1808/6857/1/final_B%26C_2010.pdf.
4. Terry Ballard, "A Graphic Interface to Online Reference Sources," *The Reference Librarian* 50 (2009): 150–158.
5. Catherine Anson and Ruth R. Connell, *E-book Collections*, SPEC Kit 313 (Washington, DC: Association of Research Libraries, 2009), 47.
6. John W. East, "'The Rolls Royce of the Library Reference Collection': The Subject Encyclopedia in the Age of Wikipedia," *Reference & User Services Quarterly* 50 (2010): 168.
7. Jason Vaughan, "Web Scale Discovery Services, Chapter 6: Differentiators and a Final Note," *Library Technology Reports* 47 (January 2011): 48–49.
8. Jeff Wisniewski, "Web Scale Discovery: The Future's So Bright, I Gotta Wear Shades," *Online*, July/August 2010, 57.
9. Judy Luther and Maureen C. Kelly, "The Next Generation of Discovery," *Library Journal*, March 15, 2011, 67.

Appendix
Reference Collection Development Policy Template

This policy template (available for download from www.alaedtions.org/ webextras/) is designed so that a librarian writing a reference collection development policy can choose one or more statements from each element of the policy and combine them to make the core of a policy. Every library has its own unique organization and policy considerations, so some editing and additional writing will be necessary to produce a completed policy that will reflect the environment and mission of the individual library.

Purpose of the Reference Collection Development Policy

1. This policy serves as one basis for making decisions about the development and maintenance of the reference collection of [name of library].
2. This policy defines the purpose of the reference collection and describes the desired scope of the collection.
3. This policy defines the criteria that should be used to determine what resources should be included in the reference collection and what resources should be excluded.
4. The purpose of the Reference Collection Development Policy is to establish general guidelines for the scope of the library reference collection and for the materials it includes to support the academic programs of [name of institution].
5. This policy will establish procedures for the acquisition of new materials and for the removal of materials, thereby ensuring the proper development and maintenance of a current and useful reference collection.
6. This policy sets forth the criteria and procedures necessary to build and maintain a reference collection that will serve the needs of [name of institution].

7. This policy supplements the library's Collection Development Policy, defining the framework for making decisions about the development and maintenance of the reference collection.

Responsibility for Reference Collection Development

1. The head of reference is responsible for the development of the reference collection.
2. The development and management of the reference collection is the joint responsibility of the reference coordinator and the collections coordinator.
3. The development and management of the reference collection is the responsibility of the head of reference, with the advice of the reference staff.
4. Every member of the reference staff bears some responsibility for the development of the reference collection, although the administrative responsibility lies with the reference coordinator.
5. The responsibility for the selection and maintenance of the reference collection is primarily the responsibility of the head of reference, with the assistance of the subject selectors.
6. All staff members who serve at the reference desk are expected to recommend materials to be added to the reference collection, although primary responsibility for shaping the collection is assigned to the reference coordinator.
7. Selection of reference materials is a shared responsibility. All members of the reference staff are expected to participate by recommending materials to be acquired, evaluating current reference resources for withdrawal from the collection and/or replacement, and performing other collection development functions as needed.
8. The final decision on what resources shall be part of the reference collection is the responsibility of the reference coordinator.
9. The head librarian is responsible for the development and maintenance of the reference collection.
10. Decisions about the content and scope of the reference collection housed in each branch are the joint responsibility of the head of reference and the head of collections at the main library. However, the head librarian of each branch library is expected to submit recommendations for desired resources.
11. The reference coordinator makes decisions about the selection, location, and deselection of both print and electronic resources, consulting with reference and/or collection development librarians as appropriate.

Purpose of the Reference Collection

1. The reference collection is meant to serve the research and information needs of the students, faculty, and staff of [name of institution].

2. The reference collection is designed to serve the research and curricular needs of the students, faculty, and staff of [name of institution].

3. The reference collection is designed to meet the research and information needs of the students and teachers of [name of school].

4. The purpose of the reference collection is to serve the informational and research needs of the population of [name of geographic area].

5. The resources in the reference collection are expected to support the teaching program of [name of institution].

6. The reference collection should provide users with quick, factual information.

7. The purpose of the reference collection is to provide a current, authoritative collection of noncirculating materials that will answer quick, factual questions on widely diverse subjects.

8. The reference collection should provide information necessary to support the work done by employees of [name of organization].

9. The resources in the reference collection have been collected to serve the informational and educational needs of library users (adults or children).

10. The resources in the reference collection are provided to support the informational and entertainment needs of the citizens of [name of geographic area].

11. The reference collection is intended to provide answers to users of the main library and to also provide reference staff with the resources necessary to assist staff at the branch libraries.

12. The purpose of the reference collection is to serve the scholarly and teaching mission of the college.

13. Most of the materials acquired for the reference collection are meant to support the curricular needs of the university. However, a more limited portion of the collection supports general informational needs of library users. These resources include career and job-hunting resources, legal information for the state and local community, information about the local region, health and wellness resources, personal finance and investment guides, etc.

14. The reference collection contains resources that provide answers to factual questions, overviews of topics, and gateways to extensive research sources. The collection also supports the daily work of library staff members who provide reference and instruction.

15. The materials in the reference collection are selected and acquired to support the informational, research, and teaching needs of [name of institution], with the emphasis on supporting the needs of the undergraduate curriculum.

16. Examples of reference materials include: encyclopedias, dictionaries, almanacs, handbooks, atlases, thesauruses, plot summaries, gazetteers, statistical sources, style manuals, telephone books, directories, legal materials, indexes and abstracts, yearbooks, etc.

17. Simply because a book is structured as a reference source does not mean that it should be shelved in the reference collection. Titles that are not considered to be useful for reference may be shelved in other parts of the library.

Target Audience(s)

1. The primary users of the reference collection are faculty, staff, and students of [name of institution].
2. The primary users of the reference collection are librarians and those seeking information in either the physical or virtual library.
3. The primary users of the reference collections are employees of [name of organization].
4. The primary users of the reference collection are expected to be members of the reference staff, on behalf of library users inside or outside the library.
5. The secondary users of the reference collection may be library users who are not affiliated with the university, such as local residents, researchers, those taking distance courses from other universities, or other library users.
6. Users of the reference collection are local residents seeking to satisfy an informational or recreational need for information.
7. The reference collection is primarily expected to serve the needs of local residents, organizations, and businesses. To a lesser extent it will also serve the needs of visitors from other library districts, students from the local college, and students taking distance courses from other colleges or universities.
8. The reference collection primarily supports the research and information needs of librarians, teaching faculty, and students. It also secondarily serves the needs of alumni and community users.

Budgeting and Funding

1. The reference services coordinator is responsible for managing the reference budget lines.
2. The head of reference is administratively responsible for the reference monographs budget line, the reference serials budget line, the reference standing orders budget line, and the reference electronic resources budget line.
3. The head of reference is not administratively responsible for any budget lines but is allowed to request that materials be purchased from budget lines administered by other library staff members.
4. The head of reference is administratively responsible for the reference budget line.

5. Reference monographs may be requested for purchase from the library's monographs budget.

6. Standing orders and/or serials for the reference collection may be requested from the library's standing orders and serials budget lines.

7. There is no budget line reserved for reference electronic resources, but these resources may be requested to be purchased from the library's general electronic resources budget lines.

8. There are no budgets reserved exclusively for materials for the reference collection. Reference materials are acquired using funds from the library's general materials budget lines.

9. Books that must be replaced because they are damaged or missing may be requested from the Replacement budget line.

10. Some reference books are received as part of the library's approval plan. The head of reference and the head of collections are jointly responsible for writing the portion of the approval plan that defines when reference books or approval slips will be received and the role they will play in the reference collection development process.

11. Shared purchases may be pursued for expensive resources.

Selection Criteria (Begin with one of these statements and then choose criteria from the lists below.)

1. Selected reference resources should be of high quality and appropriate for library users and staff. The most important factors to consider for purchases are [choose from the lists below].

2. Factors to be considered when selecting materials for the reference collection include [choose criteria from the lists below].

3. Selecting reference materials should be based on established criteria. The most important factors to be considered are [choose criteria from the list below].

Selection Criteria: General

1. Relevance to the curriculum
2. Current coverage of the topic in the collection
3. Uniqueness of coverage
4. Appropriateness for the information and research needs of the library's users
5. Authority of the author and/or publisher
6. Accuracy
7. Completeness
8. Currency
9. Age/User appropriateness
10. Accessibility

11. Geographic coverage
12. Preferred language(s)
13. Illustrations
14. Access points in other resources
15. Cost vs. quality
16. Value for the price
17. Positive reviews in standard reviewing sources
18. Inclusion in basic collection guides
19. User demand
20. Recommendations from subject selectors
21. Cost of any expected updates
22. Expense of ongoing maintenance
23. Ease of use
24. User-friendly format

Selection Criteria: Electronic Resources

1. User interface
2. Branding
3. Customization
4. Search features
5. Available indexing
6. Results display
7. Availability of full text
8. Special features
9. Ability to save, print, or e-mail results
10. Ability to export citations to bibliographic management software
11. Updates/currency
12. Availability of downloadable MARC records
13. Availability of usage data
14. Remote access
15. Mobile access
16. Cost models
17. Licensing
18. Compatibility of electronic resources with current hardware and software
19. Availability of technical support

Selection Criteria: Print Materials

1. Physical features
2. Durability
3. Visual qualities
4. Ease of use

5. Updates/currency
6. Cost models

Selection Criteria: Statements to Be Used Instead of Using a List of Criteria

Relevance of Content

1. The first consideration is the relevance of the content to the collection.
2. The primary factor to consider when selecting reference materials is its relevance to the scope of the collection.
3. The primary reason for selecting a reference resource is its utility for library users' research and information needs.
4. Usefulness to reference library staff and to library users is the primary criterion for acquiring resources for the reference collection.
5. Priority is given to resources that address issues for which information has been requested in the recent past.

Uniqueness of Coverage

1. Priority is given to resources that contain a substantial amount of information that is not found elsewhere in the library's collection, provided that information is also relevant to the research and information needs of the library's users.
2. Priority is given to resources with unique content.
3. The degree of unique content should be considered when evaluating a potential acquisition.

Authority of Author, Publisher, or Database Producer

1. The author should have excellent credentials for writing this type of resource.
2. Priority should be given to materials produced by established, reputable publishing houses that are well known for the quality of their reference books on the subject of the potential acquisition.
3. The individual entries in an encyclopedia should be signed, and each entry should include a bibliography of scholarly sources.

Accuracy

1. Factual information in the source should have a very high level of accuracy.
2. The information should display a strict attention to detail, with few typos or inaccuracies.

3. Information in reference resources should be accurate and, if possible, verifiable through the use of references.

Completeness

1. The source should cover the subject with a level of comprehensiveness that is necessary for the topic and intended use.
2. The source should cover the subject with the desired level of completeness.
3. The library prefers to purchase resources that cover a subject thoroughly.

Currency

1. Sources designed to include current information should be up to date.
2. Sources that are meant to convey the state of the art should be very current.
3. Services that index currently released sources should have a short lag time between the publication of the indexed source and its inclusion in the indexing service.
4. Up-to-date materials are given priority.

Age/User Appropriateness

1. Content and format must be appropriate to the age and/or reading level of library users.
2. All reference sources must be appropriate for [desired age or grade level].
3. The reading level of reference resources should be [enter reading level].
4. Reference materials should be appropriate for an undergraduate audience.

Accessibility

1. Reference sources must be accessible to those with visual disabilities, by providing a text-only alternative, making audio files available, or using other means.
2. Reference sources that include audio and/or video files should include closed captioning or other means of making the content accessible to those with hearing disabilities.

Geographic Coverage

1. Reference sources that cover specific geographic areas, such as travel guides, directories, and street guides, will generally be purchased for the local area only.

2. The reference collection includes resources that cover all regions of the world.
3. The materials in the reference collection emphasize coverage of [named geographic areas].
4. Resources in the reference collection emphasize the United States. However, materials on other geographic areas are purchased to support the curriculum and general reference work.

Illustrations

1. Illustrations should be appropriate to the content, contribute to users' understanding of the topic, and be of excellent quality.
2. Reference materials include many illustrations that contribute to students' understanding of the topic and are appropriate for the students' age and reading level.
3. Preference is given to sources with color illustrations.

Access Points in Other Resources

1. Preference is given to resources that are included in the library's web discovery layer service.
2. Preference is given to resources that are included in [name of resource].

Cost vs. Quality

1. The cost of a resource should be commensurate with the expected usefulness of the product.
2. Given the limited available budget, the selector should carefully weigh the potential use of the resource against the expected cost.
3. A careful comparison of the potential usefulness of a reference source with the anticipated cost should be made, particularly when considering the acquisition of expensive resources.

User Interface

1. The user interface of electronic resources should be clear, well organized, and clean.
2. The user interface should reflect the type of sources in the database and the needs of the target user population.
3. The user interface should be updated as the standards for online graphic design and user taste evolve.
4. The user interface should incorporate relevant new technologies as they become available.

Branding

1. Adequate and appropriate branding opportunities should be provided on electronic resources so the library can incorporate its name and/or logo into the user interface of the database.
2. The library should be able to add a linked logo to direct users to the online help service.
3. The library must be able to display a linked logo on the search pages that directs users to the library's online help options.

Customization

1. The library should be able to customize the user interface, including elements of the search forms, default search page, results display, export/ e-mail/printing options, etc.

Search Features

1. The variety and type of search boxes should be appropriate for the content and use of the electronic resource.
2. Available search features should be easy to use and appropriate for the content of the resource and for the user population.
3. Search operators should be appropriate for the electronic resource and should be easy to understand and use.
4. If several search pages are provided, the library should be able to change the default search page.

Available Indexing

1. The type of indexing should be appropriate for the content of the electronic resource and for the intended use of the resource.
2. Search fields should be appropriate for the content of the electronic resource and for the intended use of the resource.
3. Controlled vocabulary should be well chosen and precisely defined, and appropriate to the content and intended audience.
4. If there is a controlled vocabulary for an electronic resource, there should be an online thesaurus that is well organized, easy to use, and accessible both by searching and browsing.

Results Display

1. The content and organization of the results display should be appropriate for the type of electronic resource.

2. There should be alternative, appropriate formats for the results display. These should be easily changed by the user, and the library should be able to change the default display format.
3. The sorting method for the display should be easily determined. There should be alternative, appropriate sorting methods and the user should be able to change the sorting method.

Availability of Full Text

1. Priority may be given to databases that provide access to the full text of textual documents.
2. The extent of full text that is not currently available to library users is an important factor in selecting new electronic products.
3. When the electronic product doesn't include the full text, the ability to link to full text in other electronic products owned by the library is crucial.
4. If full text is embargoed, this must be clearly indicated within the database, and this information must be easy to find and interpret.
5. If a serial is provided full text, priority will be given to electronic products that provide a greater amount of the full text of the entire run of the serial, or of the portion of the serial that is needed by the library and its users.
6. Priority will be given to electronic products that provide the entire full text of each issue or volume of those resources included in the database, to include illustrations, bibliographies, reviews, etc.
7. Priority will be given to electronic products that provide audio files as an alternative to the full text of textual documents.

Special Features

1. Special features of electronic products will be appropriate for the content and the intended audience of the product.
2. Special features of electronic products will be carefully evaluated on a case-by-case basis.

Ability to Save, Print, or E-mail Results

1. The results of a search must be able to be printed. If the results are in color, the results should be able to be printed in color.
2. The results of a search must be able to be saved in a temporary folder.
3. If the online resource provides the ability for the user to sign in to a personal account, the user should be able to permanently save the search results and/or the search strategy so the search results can be reproduced.
4. The results of a search must be able to be e-mailed to the user or to a third party.

Ability to Export Citations to Bibliographic Management Software

1. Search results must be able to be exported to [name of bibliographic management software].
2. Search results must be able to be exported to bibliographic management software.

Updates/Currency

1. Indexing of new serial issues should be available within [time period].
2. Indexing of new newspaper issues should be available on the day they are issued.
3. Updates of the database content should be available in a timely manner.
4. When new editions of e-books are issued, the content of the previous edition should remain in the database.
5. When new editions of e-books are issued, the content of the previous edition should be deleted from the database.

Usage Data

1. Usage data should be easily available to library employees.
2. Usage data should be kept up to date and should be easily compiled by library employees.
3. Usage data should include [data elements].
4. The definition for each available data element should be available and easy to find.
5. The usage data should be COUNTER compliant.
6. The usage data should be compliant with SUSHI standards.
7. The library prefers to acquire electronic products that are COUNTER compliant and also compliant with SUSHI standards.

Remote Access

1. Electronic products must be available to all within the IP range [IP range].
2. Electronic products must work with [remote access program].
3. If there are problems with the provision of remote access, the database vendor or producer will provide technical assistance to resolve these problems.

Mobile Access

1. Priority will be given to electronic products that can be accessed on mobile devices.
2. Priority will be given to electronic products that are mobile-optimized.

3. Electronic products must be accessible on mobile devices.
4. Electronic products must be mobile-optimized.
5. Priority will be given to electronic resources that are optimized for [name of mobile device].

Cost Models

1. The cost models will be acceptable to the library.
2. The library prefers to acquire electronic resources as annual subscriptions, rather than as purchases.
3. Priority will be given to digitized historical full text resources for which the library can purchase perpetual access.
4. Cost models for electronic resources will be evaluated on a case-by-case basis.

Licensing

1. The license agreement must be acceptable to the library.
2. The license agreement should allow for materials in the database to be copied and sent on interlibrary loan.
3. The license agreement must allow for materials to be placed on reserve for classes.
4. Priority will generally be given to products that allow use by walk-in users.
5. The library prefers license agreements that allow alumni to use the product.
6. The license agreement must allow all authenticated, authorized users to access the product, regardless of physical location.
7. The license agreement must not restrict the library's ability to disclose the terms of the license agreement.
8. The license agreement must not require the library to indemnify the database vendor or producer.
9. The license agreement must be governed by the laws of [geographic entity].
10. The head of collections is authorized to negotiate all licenses.
11. All licenses are reviewed and negotiated by the electronic resources coordinator.
12. All licenses are negotiated by the head of the library.
13. Licenses are reviewed by the head of collections, in consultation with the electronic resources coordinator.
14. The library reserves the right to have all licenses reviewed by the library's general counsel.
15. Licenses will not be finalized until they have been reviewed and approved by the library's general counsel.

Technical Considerations

1. Technical assistance must be available from the database vendor or producer.
2. Adequate, timely technical assistance must be available from the database vendor or producer to resolve issues with making the product work with the library's systems.
3. Adequate, timely technical assistance should be available from the database vendor or producer to resolve any technical issues that impede the use of the electronic product.
4. The product should include relevant, adequate help pages, tutorials, and/or other forms of assistance to users.
5. Electronic resources must be compatible with currently used hardware and software.

Physical Features of Books

1. Binding should be sufficiently durable to be able to withstand normal use.
2. Binding should be strong enough and inner margins should be deep enough to allow the book to be photocopied without breaking the binding.
3. The inner margins of pages should be sufficiently deep to allow for rebinding.
4. Paper should be of good quality so that it can be rebound if necessary.

Visual Qualities

1. The typeface must be large enough and distinct enough to be easily read.
2. The typeface and paper must be of excellent quality so that they enhance the user's ability to read and understand the content of the book.
3. Illustrations must be of excellent quality.
4. Priority will be given to books that have color illustrations.

Selection Aids

The most heavily used selection aids are listed below. More specialized tools may also be used to assist the librarians in selecting useful additions to the reference collection (choose the appropriate titles from the following list):

1. Guide to Reference (www.guidetoreference.org)
2. *Reference & User Services Quarterly*
3. *Booklist*
4. *School Library Journal*
5. *Library Journal*
6. *Choice*

7. *Charleston Advisor*
8. *American Reference Books Annual*
9. ARBAOnline (http://arbaonline.com)
10. *Reference Books for Small and Medium-Sized Libraries*
11. *Walford's Guide to Reference Material*

Preferred Format

1. Serial reference publications, such as indexes, will generally be purchased as electronic products.
2. The library has a strong preference for acquiring reference materials in electronic formats.
3. The library prefers to acquire reference materials in electronic formats.
4. The library generally acquires monographic reference materials in print format.
5. The library prefers to acquire reference resources in print format.
6. The decision to acquire a reference resource in print or electronic format will be decided on the relative merits of each version.
7. Print reference materials will usually be acquired as paperbacks, unless the title is expected to be heavily used.
8. If both hardbound and paperbound editions are available, the library will generally purchase the hardbound edition for the reference collection.
9. The library has a preference for purchasing hardbound books. However, if the title is expected to be useful only for a short time, such as a book that is replaced annually by a newer edition, it should be acquired as a paperback.
10. When possible, reference resources will be purchased in electronic formats that are accessible throughout the library system.
11. Both electronic and print formats may be included in the reference collection if each offers significant advantages.
12. Electronic format is preferred. However, the print format may be purchased if an electronic format is unavailable, if the print format is much less expensive, or if the vendor's licensing terms are unacceptable.
13. The library prefers to acquire electronic formats in order to provide maximum accessibility to all users and in all physical locations within the library system.

Inclusion of Free Internet Sites

1. Except in rare cases, free Internet sites will not be included in the list of reference resources.
2. Free Internet sites will be included in the list of reference resources as appropriate.

3. Inclusion of free Internet sites in the list of reference resources will be decided on a case-by-case basis.
4. Free Internet sites will be included in the list of reference resources only when they meet the same criteria used for subscription electronic products.
5. An extensive list of free Internet sites is an integral part of the resources that are considered to be part of the reference collection.

Duplicates

1. In general, only one copy of print reference materials will be purchased for the reference collection.
2. Duplicate copies of print reference materials will be purchased only in rare cases.
3. Duplicate copies of print reference materials will be purchased only after careful consideration by the head of reference.
4. Due to high use, duplicate copies of the most popular style guides will be purchased for the reference collection.
5. Multiple copies of [name of dictionary] and [name of thesaurus] will be purchased for the reference collection.
6. For selected titles, both print and online formats may be purchased in order to provide continued accessibility if the title ceases publication or if the library loses access to the online resource.
7. Except in rare cases, reference resources will not be purchased in both print and electronic format.
8. Reference resources will not be purchased in both print and electronic formats.
9. When a reference resource is available in more than one format, the advantages and disadvantages of each format should be carefully considered before a purchase decision is finalized.
10. For selected titles, a microfiche or microfilm archival copy may be purchased, in addition to the print or online resource. This will be decided on a case-by-case basis and will be done only in very rare instances.
11. Duplicate copies of selected print reference materials may be purchased to be placed in branch libraries, as necessary.
12. The library prefers to avoid purchasing duplicate reference resources to be placed at multiple branches. Decisions about such purchases will be carefully considered on a case-by-case basis.
13. The head of reference consults with librarians at the branch libraries when necessary, in order to prevent the purchase of duplicate expensive reference resources.

14. Reference staff should avoid acquiring resources that are primarily a repackaging of content that has been previously published and is already available in the collection.

Preferred Language(s)

1. The preferred language for materials in the reference collection is English, with the exception of materials intended to assist in learning and using other languages.
2. Priority is generally given to English-language resources. However, resources in other languages may be acquired when they are superior to, provide additional coverage to, or provide unique coverage to English-language resources.
3. Priority is given to English-language resources. However, resources in other languages may be purchased if they are superior to, complement, or address subjects not covered in available English-language reference sources.
4. While most reference resources will be acquired in English, selected resources will be purchased in [name of language].
5. Most reference resources will be acquired in English and/or [name of language].
6. The reference collection should include a general encyclopedia in each of the languages taught at [name of institution].
7. Foreign-language resources will be limited to those that support the study of the languages taught at [name of institution].
8. Reference resources should be purchased to serve the reference and information needs of the population of [geographic area], to include the following languages: [list of languages].
9. Most reference resources will be acquired in English. However, the reference collection includes an extensive collection of dictionaries and other language sources that reflect the wide diversity of languages used by the library's users.
10. Reference resources in all languages will be considered for acquisition, reflecting the wide diversity of languages spoken by the library's users.
11. Reference resources in all languages will be considered for acquisition, reflecting the wide diversity of languages spoken, taught, or read by faculty, staff, and students at [name of institution].

Circulation

1. The print reference collection is a noncirculating collection.
2. Print materials in the reference collection do not circulate.

3. Since books in the reference collection are expected to be used frequently by librarians and/or library users, they are designated to be noncirculating.
4. Print materials in the reference collection may circulate only with permission of the head of reference.
5. Print materials in the reference collection may circulate only with permission of a reference librarian.
6. Print materials in the reference collection may circulate only with permission of a member of the reference staff.
7. Print materials in the reference collection may circulate for [specify time period].
8. Most print materials in the reference collection circulate. The volumes that do not circulate are marked with a *Do Not Circulate* label or stamp.
9. Most print materials in the reference collection circulate. The volumes that do not circulate are marked with a *Library Use Only* label or stamp.
10. Print materials in the ready reference collection do not circulate.

Treatment of Specific Resource Groups

1. The library does not normally include consumer-oriented publications in the reference collection. Examples of these publications include: travel guides, genealogy resources, test preparation guides, hobby guides (coins, stamps, antiques, etc.), auto mechanics manuals, and personal finance.
2. In general, reference-type resources with a very narrow focus, such as encyclopedias about a single person, will not be purchased for the reference collection.
3. The library does not purchase highly technical or scholarly resources for the reference collection.
4. The library will purchase almanacs, yearbooks, gazetteers, and place-specific encyclopedias only for [name geographic locations].
5. In general, only the most recent edition [or specify the number of years or editions] of almanacs and yearbooks will be retained for the reference collection. Earlier editions may be sent to the circulating collection or remote storage.
6. Directories will be acquired only if similar information is not elsewhere available.
7. Quotation books will be acquired only if the source citations are sufficiently complete.
8. The reference collection does not include textbooks or other curriculum materials.
9. The reference collection does not include travel guides.
10. Travel guides in the reference collection are regularly updated to support faculty research in other locations and student study abroad.
11. Guides to individual works, such as *Cliffs Notes*, are not purchased for the reference collection.

12. The library no longer purchases concordances for any work that is available in a full-text electronic format.
13. The reference collection does not include genealogical resources. These are generally purchased for the local history and genealogy collection.
14. Bibliographies for narrow topics will no longer be purchased for the reference collection but rather will be placed in the circulating collection.
15. Only bibliographies on major topics will be purchased for the reference collection. Bibliographies on narrow subjects or individual authors will be acquired for the circulating collection. An exception may be made for bibliographies on topics that are in high demand or on major literary figures, such as Shakespeare.
16. Larger, more substantial foreign-language dictionaries will be purchased for the reference collection. However, pocket or student dictionaries will be purchased only for the circulating collection.
17. The reference collection includes collective guides to colleges and universities in the United States or to major universities worldwide, volumes that compare programs at different colleges and universities, and financial aid guides. The collection does not contain guides to individual colleges and universities.
18. Guides to microform collections owned by the library should all be housed in the reference collection.
19. Reference resources for [name of subject] will not be purchased for inclusion in the reference collection. These materials will instead be purchased for the [name of special collection or branch library].
20. The ready reference collection, shelved near the reference desk, includes a limited number of resources that are frequently used to answer reference and information questions.

Resource Sharing

1. The library prefers to acquire electronic reference resources rather than print, as they facilitate resource sharing among library branches.
2. Decisions about which electronic reference products to purchase will include careful consideration of how any proposed acquisition might overlap with resources provided through the library's consortia.
3. The library gives priority to the acquisition of electronic resources through the library's consortia in order to make the best use possible of the library's limited budget.

Collection Maintenance

1. The reference coordinator is administratively responsible for the maintenance of the reference collection.
2. The access services department is responsible for shelving print materials and performing other collection maintenance functions.

3. Maintenance of the print and electronic reference collection is shared among the head of reference, the head of access services, and the head of technical services.

Weeding and Reviewing the Collection

1. As new editions of print materials are received, older editions are frequently removed from the reference collection. Older editions may be sent to the circulating collection or storage, if they have historical value.
2. The head of reference has primary responsibility for planning and administering the review of the reference collection.
3. The head of collections and the head of reference will jointly plan and manage a review of the reference collection every [specify time period].
4. Reference resources will be evaluated by both reference staff and collection development staff.
5. Reviewing the reference collection is the responsibility of the reference librarians, but other library and nonlibrary entities may be consulted, as needed.
6. Each subject selector should review the relevant portion of the reference collection every year to recommend withdrawals and updates.
7. The reference collection is weeded periodically so that it will be continue to be current and useful.
8. The reference collection is weeded periodically to ensure that it will remain current and authoritative.
9. The space allocated to the print reference collection remains static. Therefore, the collection must be regularly reviewed, and books that are no longer needed for the collection should be removed so that the collection can be shelved within this designated space.
10. The reference collection is reviewed periodically so that materials that are no longer necessary can be removed from the collection, so that the collection remains current, and so that areas needing to be expanded can be identified.
11. General guidelines for reviewing the reference collection include the appropriateness of the material for the collection; in-house use statistics; age and currency of the information; physical condition of the resource; accuracy of the information; availability of a newer edition or newer comparable resource; and duplication of information.
12. The print reference collection will be weeded every [time period].
13. The print reference collection will be continuously reviewed.
14. Policies and procedures for weeding the reference collection are included in a separate document.

Policy Revision

1. The Reference Collection Development Policy will be revised every [time period]. The head of reference has primary responsibility for accomplishing this revision.
2. The Reference Collection Development Policy will be revised every [time period] by a committee to consist of the head of collections, the head of reference, and three members of the reference staff.
3. The Reference Collection Development Policy will be revised every [time period] by the reference staff and will be approved by the library governing board.
4. The periodic revision of the Reference Collection Development Policy must be approved by the dean of the library.
5. The periodic revision of the Reference Collection Development Policy must be approved by the governing board.

Index